逮捕の要領

How to Arrest Suspects

An Illustrated Guide to Jujutsu and Hojo

Yokohama & Osaka

Includes:

Using Jujutsu to Disarm

Hojo Rope Binding

Interrogating & Transporting Suspects

Guarding at a Jail

Japanese Police Manual

Translated by Eric Shahan

Translator's Introduction

This is a translation of two illustrated police manuals published in 1941. They were stamped *Not to be shared outside the police department* and were probably used in conjunction with training seminars. The training manuals are from two of the biggest cities in Japan, Osaka and Yokohama. The manuals contain information on how to interview people, search suspects and subdue violent suspects with Jujutsu. This includes facing off against criminals armed with weapons. Finally, there is an introduction to Hojo, rope binding techniques, which were used instead of handcuffs.

The full titles of the two books are:

Yokohama Guide:

不審尋問と逮捕の要領

付録

不審者の誰何尋問

被疑者の同行

留置場看守

捕縄術の要領

How to Question Suspicious Persons and Arrest Them
With Additional Material : How to Escort Suspects, How to Guard Prisoners in Jail and Hojo Jutsu

Osaka Guide:

逮捕の要領

付録

捕縄術の要領

How to Arrest
Additional Material: Outline of Hojo Jutsu, Binding With Rope Techniques

The Hojo, police rope, sections were identical in both pamphlets so it will only be reproduced once.

Jujutsu Techniques

For the Jujutsu techniques the instructions refer to "corners," as in "…reverse the Attacker's wrist upward until he falls on his front right corner." This was apparently a common way both to describe action and to give instructions to trainees.

An example of how this teaching method was used can be found in the book *The Guiding Principles of Judo* 柔道指針, published in 1936. The section is titled, "Making Your Opponent" describes how this method was introduced. Below is the page from the original book:

（イ）　自己の作り

自分の技を相手に掛けるのに、最も都合のよい姿勢及び位置にすることである。

（ロ）　相手の作り

安定せる相手の體を、不安定な姿勢にすることで、換言すれば、相手をして轉び易い姿勢にすることである。

相手を作るには、次の八方向が最も適當である。

一、眞前　二、右前隅　三、左前隅　四、右横　五、左横　六、眞後　七、右後隅　八、左後隅

以上を總稱して「八方の作り」と云ふ。

作りの方向を云ひ現す時には、相手の體を標準にして云ふのである。

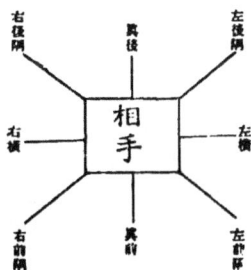

右後隅　眞後　左後隅
右横　　相手　　左横
右前隅　眞前　左前隅

English translation of the previous page

When you have an opponent who is in a stable position you need to destabilize him and force him into a position that will enable you to topple him easily.

To "Make an Opponent" it is best to use eight directions.

1. Directly in front
2. Right front corner
3. Left front corner
4. Right Side
5. Left Side
6. Directly behind
7. Right back corner
8. Left back corner.

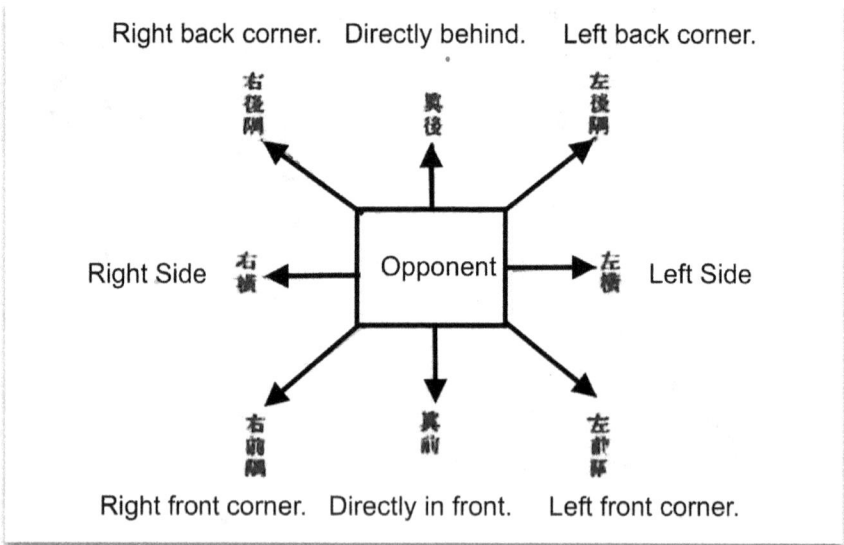

Right back corner. Directly behind. Left back corner.

右後隅　真後　左後隅

Right Side　右横　Opponent　左横　Left Side

右前隅　真前　左前隅

Right front corner. Directly in front. Left front corner.

This is generally referred to as Happo Tsukuri 八方作り "Making the Eight Directions" When directions are called out, this is how it relates to your opponent's body.

Yokohama Guide
Outline of How to Question Suspects and Arrest People
December 1st Showa 16 (1941)

24~3

昭和十六年十二月一日

不審尋問と逮捕の要領

部外秘

不審尋問と逮捕の要領

（附錄 捕繩術の要領 不審者の誰何尋問 被疑者の同行 留置場看守 等に關する心得）

神奈川縣防犯協會

Not to be shared outside the office

How to Question Suspicious Persons
&
Arrest Suspects

- **How to Conduct Interviews of Suspicious Characters**
  - **How to Escort Suspects**
  - **How to Guard Prisoners in Jail**
    - **Other Topics**

Additional Material: Outline of Hojo Jutsu, Rope Techniques

Published by the Kanagawa Prefecture Crime Prevention Society

序

武道は我が國民修養道として重んぜられ、往昔武士の能く之を勵み以て武士道精神の昂揚を圖り、國民性の涵養に資したのであつて、世の平亂、時代の推移を問はず齊しく練磨せざるべからざる要道にして、殊に警察に職を奉する者、本道の研究練磨の要極めて切なるは言ふまでもない。

即ち警察官は日夜不眠不休寒暑を冒し、櫛風沐雨の中に激務に服する者たるが故に頑健なる體力を要し、又時ありてか水火を踏み兇暴に抗し闘爭に對せざるべからざるが故に勇猛果敢能く難に處して捜まず危に臨みて逡巡せず、確固不拔の不勤心を涵養し、苟も不遏兇暴の徒輩を敢然として捕拿制御し能く之を處理するを得て初めて其の職務を完遂し得るものなりと信ずるものにして、故に警察官に武術修業の必要なる所以が存すと言ふべきである。

殊に警察官として職務の完遂に直接役立つべき『武技』の體得即ち『警察實用武術』の正しき基礎をつくることは職務の執行上極めて肝要なりと認めらるゝものにして、這般柔道敎師と警察部警務課及刑事課の各保長を以て警察武術研究會を設け、數次に亙り研究の結果案が成案を見るに至つたのである。其の『技』の種類は數種に過ぎざるも之を反復練習し其の正しき基礎をつくり之に成熟するならば機に臨み變に應じ必ずや役立つものがあると信ずる。要はお互の熱意ある練習に俟つのみで、茲に研究會に參與した一人として其の趣旨を述ぶる次第である。

昭和十六年十一月二十五日

警務課長　奥　田　信　雄

Introduction
By Police Chief Okuda Nobuo

Our country places a lot of emphasis on developing martial arts skills. Long ago, Samurai would train martial arts intensely to build their Bushido spirit. Intense training in martial arts is also a way to develop the Japanese people's patriotism. It doesn't matter if the world is trending towards peace or trending towards disorder, it is essential that you maintain your readiness. It would be a grave error to allow your training to lapse instead of continuing to polish and refine it.

Martial arts training is particularly important for those serving as police officers since an officer must be adept at all aspects of martial arts, down to the minutest detail. As an officer, you must be on duty day and night without sleep and without respite and you must toil while struggling through wind and rain. Thus, having a healthy and strong body is essential. As a police officer, you will sometimes have to wade through water and other times pass through flames. Sometimes you may be forced to meet violence with violence, thus it is important for you to be both brave and assertive, and never bend or hesitate when encountering a dangerous situation. Moreover, it is imperative that you develop a determined spirit and indomitable will.

Officers must be skilled at subduing, restraining and using Hojo, the police rope, on any violent or aggressive suspect they encounter. To gain confidence, you need to believe you have the ability to successfully arrest a suspect for the first time. This course will present the martial arts skills that are necessary.[1]

The purpose of this course is to teach 「Bugi 武技」 martial arts techniques that are practical and can be applied in the field, to allow you to successfully facilitate an arrest. This course will allow participants to acquire a solid foundation in 「*Keisatu Jitsuyo Bujutsu* 警察実用武術」 Practical Police Martial Arts, which is an essential skill for the execution of your duties.

---

[1] This seems to indicate this book was part of a lecture and practical training course for new police officers.

序

武道は我が國民修養道として重んぜられ、往昔武士の能く之を勵み以て武士道精神の昂揚を圖り、國民性の涵養に資したのであつて、世の平亂、時代の推移を問はず齊しく練磨せざるべからざる要道にして、殊に警察に職を奉ずる者、本道の研究練磨の要極めて切なるは言ふまでもない。

即ち警察官は日夜不眠不休寒暑を冒し、櫛風沐雨の中に激務に服する者なるが故に頑健なる體力を要し、又時ありてか水火を踏み兇暴に抗し鬪爭に對せざるべからざるが故に勇猛果敢能く難に處して撓まず危に臨みて遂巡せず、確固不抜の不勵心を涵養し、苟も不遜兇暴の徒輩を敢然として捕拏制抑し能く之を處理するを得て初めて其の職務を完遂し得るものなりと信ずるものにして、玆に警察官に武術修業の必要なる所以が存すと言ふべきである。

殊に警察官として職務の完遂に直接役立つべき『武技』の體得即ち『警察實用武術』の正しき基礎をつくることは職務の執行上極めて肝要なりと認めらるゝものにして、遂毅柔道敎師と警察部警務課及刑事課の各保長を以て警察武術研究會を設け、數次に亘り研究の結果之が成案を見るに至つたのである。其の『技』の種類は數種に過ぎざるも之を反復練習し其の正しき基礎をつくり之に成熟するならば機に臨み變に應じ必ずや役立つものがあると信ずる。要はお互の熱意ある練習に俟つのみで、玆に研究會に參與した一人として其の趣旨を述ぶる次第である。

昭和十六年十一月二十五日

警務課長　奧　田　信　雄

To facilitate this training we have set up a 「*Keisatu Bujutsu Kenkyukai* 警察武術研究会」 Police Martial Arts Research Society comprised of Judo instructors, military police officers, police detectives as well as police section chiefs. The members of the group shared their training procedures with each other and consolidated them into a training program.

When developing the techniques to be introduced to police officers, this group decided to limit the number of 「*Waza* 技」 Techniques so that by means of 「*Hanpuku Renshu* 反復練習」 Repeated Training of the Same Technique, a solid foundation in the basics will form. If you thoroughly train the fundamental techniques outlined here then, when you encounter a violent situation, you will be able to respond and adapt to any sudden changes that occur.

The most important part of this training is being passionate and involved. This applies for both teachers and learners. Clearly those of you attending this seminar have such a desire.

November 25th
Showa 16 (1941)

序

犯罪事件が發生して、それが檢擧されなかつたとしたら、社會民衆の不安と實害といふものは決して尠しとせざるのみならず、警察の威信を失墜すること亦大なりと言はねばならぬのであるが、然し犯罪の檢擧の苦勞と勞力と言ふことは並大抵のことではない。多數民衆の中から容疑の有無を見分けるのであるから平素犯罪捜査に專從する者にとつても容易なことではないのみならず、犯人は働く迄も自己の犯罪を隱蔽しようとし又彼等の奸智は普通人の數倍も發達して居る。そして隙さへあれば逃走を企てようとする。此の不逞の徒輩を對象として能く其の取扱に過ちなく警察官としての職務を完遂するには單に有形的束縛を以て安心するが如きことなく警察官の態度に心服せしめ所謂無形的束縛を加ふるの心構こそ最も肝要である。

玆に警察實用武術として逮捕に付ての基本要領が示され、更に又不審尋問、救護者の同行及留置場看守等に關する心得を第一線警察官各位の爲に編まれたことは必ずや好個の指導書たり得ることを信ずるのである。

昭和十六年十一月二十五日

刑事課長　小　林　要　藏

Introduction
By Head Detective Kobayashi Yozo

If a crime were to occur and it was not investigated, the repercussions would be far reaching. Not only would it be damaging to society and cause citizens to become fearful, but it would also mean that police would lose their respect and authority.

However, the process of investigating crimes, finding the suspect and arresting them requires no small amount of effort. Searching for a suspect amongst a sea of average citizens is a difficult process, even for a seasoned investigator. In addition, criminals are adept at concealing the fact that they are involved in anything illegal. Further, their involvement in criminality means they have developed clever deceptive tactics that are far beyond those of a normal person.

If discovered, these criminals have every intention of trying to escape. Nevertheless, when responding to these lawless people, a police officer must avoid employing excessive force. To facilitate this, police do not rely solely on tangible, physical methods of restraint to conduct an arrest safely and effectively. Police officers also use the respect and admiration felt by citizens towards police in general. The most important aspect of policing is the presence you project as an officer of the law, something that is intangible, yet still serves as a method of restraint on a suspect.

This book presents a practical approach to teaching the fundamentals of police martial arts arresting techniques. In addition, it contains a chapter on how to question suspicious persons, how to escort prisoners, as well as how to guard prisoners at jail. In short this is an essential collection that has been made from the perspective of police officers and will make an excellent resource and instruction manual.

November 25th
Showa 16 (1941)

不審尋問と逮捕の要領

一、緒言

強健なる身體と不撓なる氣力とに重點を置き以て警察使命の遂行に遺憾なからしむるを期すると共に之に術力を伴はしめて三位一體の所謂警察實用武術の要道に徹し事に臨んで沈着にして然も敏捷なる動作の熟練に依つて更に之が「實用」又は「用」の價値と結びつき警察官吏たるの任務を遂行せしめることが極めて肝要である。

今回警察實用武術として逮捕術に關して研究し其の基本として數種の形が考案されたのである。固より千變萬態である實際の場合の總てに形通りに嵌めるべきものではないが、常に絶へざる工夫と練習に依つて堪能に通ずるならば、其處に自ら「技」を修業する心棒へが生れ、精練された「技」は咄嗟の場合に於て克く機に臨み變に應じ何れかの「技」が必ずや役立ち得るものである。されば平素反覆演練し所謂習ひ性と興に成るの域に達するならば一旦危急の秋にも周章度を失することなき沈着且つ敏速なる動作の練熟に至るべきは容易であると信ずるのである。而して修練の基本として手の握力、腕力や關節や筋肉を強靱ならしむる爲め、基本の形から順序を逐よて之を行ひ、運足や體の變化も共に體得されて、初めて其の基礎が出來て應用も容易になるので

一

How to Question Suspicious Persons and Make Arrests
1. Initial Remarks

Ideally, a police officer will have a strong and healthy body combined with an unbending force of will. This will allow him to execute his duties without uncertainty. Those physical and mental traits combined with refined practical skills form a trinity within the body of a police officer. By practical martial arts I am referring to the *Keisatsu Jitsuyo Bujutsu* 警察実用武術 Practical Police Martial Arts, which are ingrained in police officers, enabling them to calmly and decisively handle any situation. These skills are valuable because they are both practical 「実用」 and have an ease of application 「用」 which enable officers to execute their duties.

Practical Police Martial Arts are absolutely a fundamental part of police training. This course is the result of research into *Taiho Jutsu* 「逮捕術」 Traditional Japanese Arresting Techniques. This course is a series of techniques based on this research.

It goes without saying that in a fight, one person can attack another person in 1000 different ways and the other person can respond with 10,000 different defenses. In a real fight, the strikes and defenses will never match those of a technique that you learned. However, by making training *Waza* 「技」 Techniques an integral part of your life and developing new ways to test your skill, you will ingrain the ability to react effectively. Through rigorous training, you will develop an indomitable spirit and your Waza will be ready at a moment's notice.

Further, if you dedicate yourself to training, your technique will become adaptable to any situation or variable you encounter. Thus repeatedly drilling these techniques will build the foundation for learning that will enable you to develop expert-level skill. By doing so you will be able to, without a doubt, calmly and successfully extract yourself from a life-or-death situation.

The fundamentals of this art include methods for improving grip strength, arm strength as well as ways to make the joints and muscles strong and resilient. Therefore the program should be followed in order. Leg exercises are important because those are what you use to position your body. By training the fundamentals you will become able to employ the techniques effectively.

二、不審尋問から逮捕迄

不審尋問は警察官の第六感により不審と認めたるものを尋問するものなるも、此の第六感は幾多の苦い経験とそして自己の職務を天職と心得、報国の信念と責任感に燃え、精励恪勤常に積極的に任務の遂行に当ることに依り其の成果を得るものであつて何人にも容易に望み得るものではない。又最初より犯人なりや否やは不明であり、殊に犯罪者は努めて常人と異らざる態度を装ふを常とするを以て一見して直ちに容疑の有無を見分けることは尚更困難であつて、平素犯罪捜査に専従する者にとつても容易な業ではない。況んや一般警察官の深夜勤務又は警急配備等に於て通行人を一々選別して尋問せんとするが如きは到底望んでも出来ないことである。

従つて特に犯罪容疑なきことの明白なる場合を除き服装容貌の如何に不拘必ず一応尋問することは已むを得ない所で、不審尋問の網に掛る者は犯罪者よりも善良なる者が其の数に於て遙に多いのが実際であり、其の容疑者には仲々出会はない。

従つて動もすれば心身に油断を生じ、偶々不良の徒輩に遭遇したる場合不慮の兇害を受け或は重要犯人を逸脱せしむる等の事態を惹起する様な例を尠しとしないのである。

固より良民に対する警察官の言語動作は穏和叮嚀なるを要し、如何なる場合にも初めから容疑者に対する様な言動は許されない。又仮令容疑者なりと雖も兇悪性又は抵抗の虞あるもの〻外は粗

ある。

II. From Questioning a Suspicious Person to Making an Arrest

The decision to question a person occurs because something triggers the sixth sense of a police officer, and he becomes suspicious. This leads to the person being interviewed. The source of this sixth sense is the many and varied difficult experiences you endured in the course of your duty. It is something you understand is part of your duty in this vocation, one that fills you with a fierce patriotism and sense of responsibility.

In order to be an effective officer you must not only be diligent in your work but act proactively in the execution of your duties, something that is beyond the capacity of most people. Be that as it may, as you begin questioning a person it won't be clear at the outset whether the person is a criminal or not. Add to that the fact that a criminal will take pains to adopt the attitude of a regular citizen. This means immediately discerning criminality would be difficult even for a detective, whose job it is to investigate crime. Expecting an average officer who is working late in the night, or has suddenly been called to duty for an emergency, to make such a distinction as crowds of people pass by is somewhat unrealistic.

So, barring the rare cases where the criminality is clearly apparent, no matter what clothing a person is wearing or how they appear, your duty is to question them. If a dragnet has been set up and the mission is to question all the people in an area, then the vast majority of the people you encounter will be good citizens. This means it will prove quite difficult to find the suspect or suspects.

Thus there is a tendency for officers to become lax in body and mind as the work progresses. In this case, when officers do, by chance, finally encounter a ruffian they can, unfortunately, be injured or allow a serious criminal to escape. Examples of such instances are not rare.

It is essential that officers are unfailingly polite when dealing with good citizens. It is unforgivable to start an interaction by speaking and acting harshly as if the person were a suspect. Further even if the person you are questioning is a suspect and they are resisting, if you use rough language it will only further exacerbate the situation, resulting in a waste of energy. It is important to keep this in mind.

暴に亙り、相手方を激昂せしめて無用なる力を加ふるが如きことのなき様留意すべきは勿論なるも深夜の通行者中には往々兇悪なる徒輩も亦尠くないのであるから此の點深く留意し、何時如何なる場合にも不覺を取らざる丈けの周到なる注意を拂ひ逮捕の目的を果し職務の完遂を期さなければならないのである。

三、不審尋問の氣構

不審尋問をなさんとする場合、警察官は質疑應答のみに捉はれて被尋問者の擧動に注意を缺くが如きことなく相手方は常に

（一）戎器兇器の類を所持して居るかも知れない

（二）何時抵抗するかも知れない

（三）隙があれば逃走を企て或は容疑物件を抛棄するかも知れない

（四）詐言を以て警察官を韜晦化すかも知れない

斯様に周到なる豫想の下に何時でも之に應ずる丈の心構を以て臨むことが必要である。而して被尋問者と自己との位置の關係は被尋問者が逃走を企て、或は危害を加ふるに最も不利なる位置に於て被尋問者に接近し、其の間何等の動作をも爲す間隙を與へざること必要とすべきも、人は概ね右利なるを以て尋問する場合は相手の右を制する爲め原則として相手方の右側に接近し、機先を制して相手方の抵抗の餘地を與へざる氣魄を示し、常に其の氣配に注意し、咄嗟の抵抗に備へ

三

When questioning people passing by late at night it is not uncommon for an officer to encounter a violent thug. Thus the previous point is something to keep in mind.

No matter where you are or what time it is, do not allow yourself to be caught unaware. You must maintain an awareness of your surroundings as you strive to achieve your goal and fulfill your duty by arresting suspects.

III. Important Considerations When Questioning a Suspicious Person

When questioning a suspicious person you should not focus solely on the answers to your questions and but also note how the interviewee is acting. In particular, you should keep in mind:

1. This person could have a weapon or other dangerous object
2. This person could start to resist at any time
3. If given an opportunity, this person could try to escape or destroy incriminating evidence
4. This person may lie or otherwise try to deceive the police officer

It is essential that an officer maintain an awareness of all these possible outcomes and be prepared to respond to any of them. Further, as a police officer, you should be conscious of how you position yourself in relation to the person you are interviewing. In particular, it is important to not position yourself unfavorably to the person you are interviewing. You do not want to give the interviewee an opportunity suddenly make an escape attempt or try and attack you. Ensure you are standing close enough to the interviewee to not give them any room to act.

Generally speaking, people are right-handed, so in principle, when questioning a person, you should stand on their right side in order to exercise control over that hand. Further, by approaching from the right side you stifle any move they were planning and make it difficult for them to react to your imposition on their space.

You should strictly maintain your awareness in case the person you are interviewing suddenly tries to resist.

つゝ、先づ第一に身體の檢査より始め戎兇器、臟物、犯罪用具、身體衣服の異狀等の發見に努め後適當なる尋問の追究に依つて之が答辯と其の態度に曖昧不審の點なきやを判斷すべきである。所が從來の不審尋問の要領を見るに第一に住所、氏名、行先等の形式的なる尋問から始め後身體檢査に移る者がある。是は相手方に兇器を使用せしむるの準備と機會を與へることゝなり、非常な危險を伴ふ虞があるから特に注意を要する點である。又被尋問者に所持品を取出さしむるが如きことは極めて危險である。

四、練習の要領

練習に當つては適格に其の要領を會得すべきを念とし常に誠實眞摯なる努力を積むべきことが緊要である。故に指導者は技の種類に從ひ其の目的及方法を懇切に説明し、共の要領を會得せしめ且つ實施の經過竝に結果を綿密に檢査し批評を與へ、習熟するに從ひ被縛者をして抵抗又は繩拔を爲さしむる等實用に適合せしむるを念とすべきである。

而して演練を行ふに當りては二人を一組とし之を縛者、被縛者に分け、左の號令を下し秩序正しく練習するを可とする。

一、準備運動

逮捕の基本要領に依り次の號令を以て行ふ

「何々」用意

四

The first thing you should do when questioning a person is to begin by searching them for weapons or dangerous objects, stolen goods, tools a criminal would use, or suspicious clothing. Following this, ask appropriate questions and if you feel a hint of doubt in the answers you get or in the interviewee's attitude you should follow up and make an appropriate judgement.

While we are on this subject, the primary questions to ask a suspicious person you stopped are, and this may be obvious: The person's address, name, destination as well as other standard questions. Following that you would conduct a body search if deemed necessary.[2]

IV. How to Train

It is of the upmost importance that your training be done in a competent manner and that you study this program rigorously. Training should be conducted with a seriousness of purpose with all participants striving to steadily build their skills. Therefore the instructor will carefully explain the method and objective of each Waza, or technique. Having developed a thorough grasp of the material and been able to pass a detailed examination of your skill, your ingrained technique will enable you to successfully subdue any violent suspect you encounter and secure him with rope. Understand that the goal of this training is to develop your ability to employ Practical Police Martial Arts.

For training purposes, officers will be split into pairs with one person playing the role of the Bakusha 縛者, the person tying the knots, with the other officer playing the role of the Hi-Bakusha 被捕者, the person being tied.

---

[2] Previously the author recommended searching the suspect first.

二、逮捕の要領

『何々技』　捕縄用意

『始め』

練習に於て縛者完全に施縄を終りたるときは姿勢を正し

『終り』

と呼び指導者に報告するものとす

『止め』

の號令にて施縄を解き舊位置に復す

始め

止め

直れ

五

1. Warm-up Exercises

According to the Outline of Arresting Techniques, these exercises are done with the following commands:

「Exercise Name」 *Yoi!* Ready
Hajime! Begin
Yame! Stop
Naore! Return to Your Initial Stance

2. Arresting Techniques

「Technique Name」 *Yoi!* Ready
Prepare your Hojo Arresting Rope

Hajime! Begin :
The person in the role of the arresting officer completes the designated tie and then stands at attention.

Owari! End:
At this command you present your prisoner tied up with the technique in question.

Yame! Stop :
At this command you untie the ropes and return to your original starting position.

逮捕の基本要領

要目／區分	準	
	準備運動體形に集れ	(1) 握力 用意
圖示	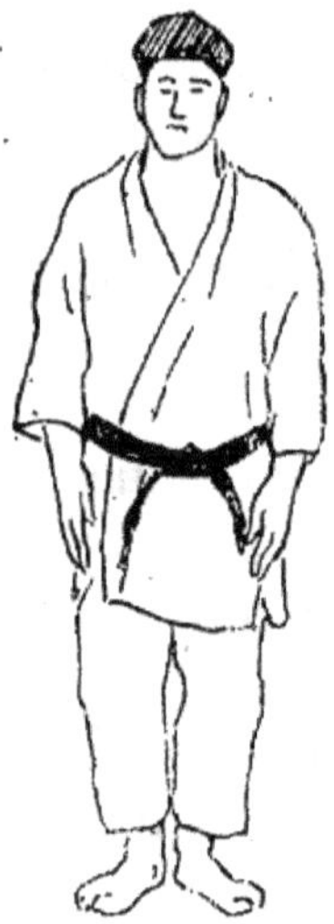 1	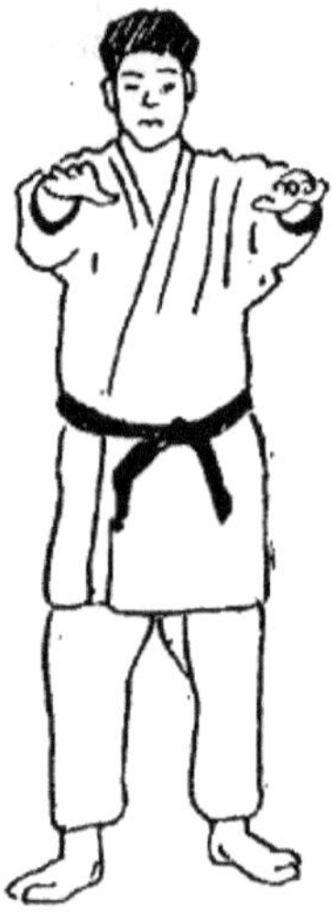 2
要領	上圖の如く稍々不動の姿勢となる	左足を約半歩横に開き自然體となり 兩手を前面水平に上げ指先を伸す

六

Fundamental Arresting Techniques
An Illustrated Guide
Warm-up Exercises

1. *Akuryoku no Undo*
Improving Grip Strength 1/2

As Illustration 1 shows, you should be in a relaxed Fudo Shisei, or Immovable Stance. Students should gather and stand in this position

At the command of *Yoi!* Prepare! take a half step out with your left foot. This means you will be in Shizen Tai, Natural Stance. Raise both hands in front of you, parallel to the ground and extend your fingers. This is shown in Illustration 2.

運	の
め　　　　　止	め　　　　　始

運

止め

上圖の如く用意の際と同様の姿勢と
なる

の

始め

堅く握り緊める
（繰返すこと各自十回以上）

七

Akuryoku no Undo
Improving Grip Strength: Steps 3 & 4

Stop!   *Begin!*

At the command of *Hajime!* Begin! squeeze your hands into tight fists. (Each person should repeat this 10 times or more.) This is shown in the third illustration.

As Illustration 4 shows, at the command of *Yame!* Stop! you return to the stance shown in Illustration 2.

備	
の　　　足　（2）	動
意　　　用	れ　　　直
 1	 5
上圖の如く兩手を腰に取る	左足を引付け兩足を揃へて最初の姿勢となる

Akuryoku no Undo
Improving Grip Strength: Step 5

Ready!   *Return!*

At the command of *Naore!* Return! pull your left foot in so that both feet are together, therefore returning to your initial stance. This is shown in Illustration 5.

2. *Ashi no Undo*
Leg Exercises: Step 1

At the command of *Yoi!* Prepare! place your hands on your hips as shown.

運

始　め　　　　　　　　始　め

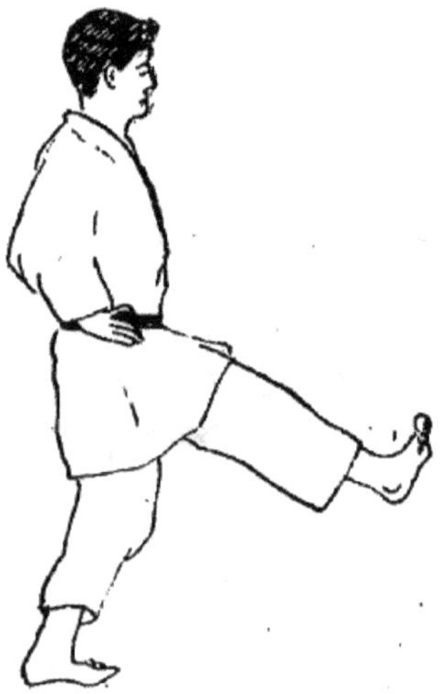

3　　　　　　　　　　2

逆に後方を踵骨で蹴る
（連續前後四回以上繰返す）

上圖の如く右蹠頭で素早く前方を蹴
る
（連續前後四回以上繰返す）

九

Ashi no Undo
Leg Exercises: Step 2 & 3

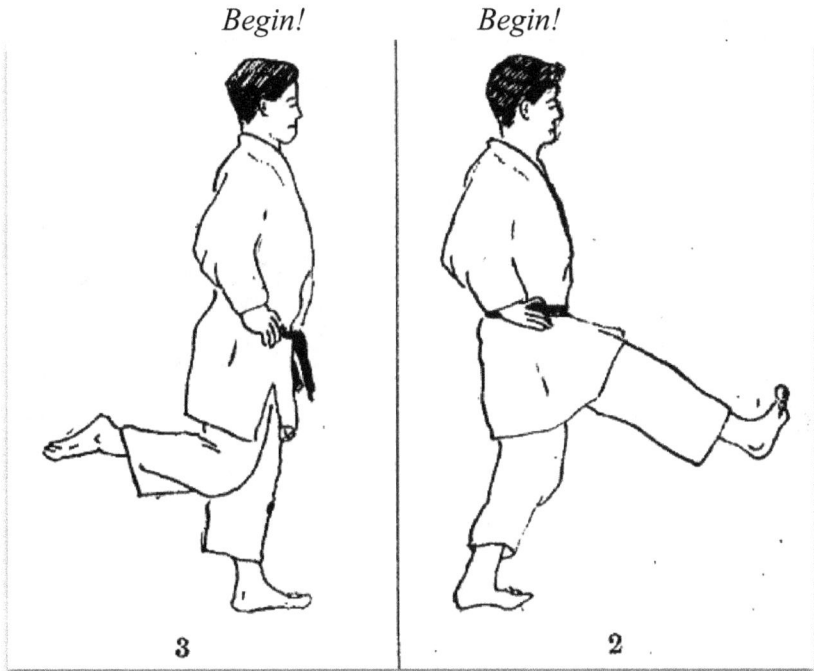

Begin!   *Begin!*

3   2

As Illustration 2 shows, rapidly swing the bottom of your right foot forward in a kick. (Return your foot to the starting position then kick forward again, keeping the motion continuous. Do this at least four times.)

As shown in Illustration 3, when kicking behind you, strike with your heel. (Return your foot to the starting position and then kick again, keeping the motion continuous. Do this at least four times.)

運

動

れ　直	め　止
5	4
兩手を下し最初の姿勢となる	上圖の如く用意の際と同様の姿勢となる

一〇

Leg Exercises: Step 4 & 5

Return!   *Stop!*

As Illustration 4 shows, at the command Stop! you return to *Yoi*, Ready Stance.

Illustration 5 shows how you lower both hands to return to your starting stance.

ほ　　　　　　　手　（3）	
め　　　　始	意　　　用

2

1

上行ふ）

突き上げる氣持を以て左右十回以

（此の場合　全身に力を入れ體諸共

上げる

を入れ握られた手を放さぬ樣に突き

上圖の如く拳を固め手首にぐつと力

輕く握る

上圖の如く左足を半歩横へ開き手を

3. *Tehodoki*
Freeing Your Hand: Step 1 & 2

Begin!   *Ready!*

As Illustration 1 shows, first step a half step to the side with your left foot and squeeze your hands into loose fists.

Then squeeze your right hand into a tight fist and put power in your wrist. Swing your right arm upward while not trying to use too much force as you don't want to cause the person who has grabbed your wrist to let go.

(At this point you should put power in your whole body, so that when you strike upwards, it is as if every part of your body is moving. Practice at least ten times on the right and then ten times on the left.)

動	
き れ 直	ど め 止

| 4 | 3 |

左足を引付け兩足を揃へて最初の姿勢となる

上圖の如く用意の際と同様の姿勢となる

一二

3. *Tehodoki*
Freeing Your Hand: Steps 3 & 4

Return!   *Stop!*

As Illustration 3 shows, at the command Stop! you return to *Yoi*, Ready Stance.

Illustration 4 shows how you have lowered both hands and returned to your starting stance.

第一技

兩

2

1

手ほどきの動作に依り右足を相手の右足先に近く踏出し同時に（圖の如く）右手甲の上より兩手で指骨を攬み手首を捻り小手を制す

上圖の如く正面より兩手を握らせる

一三

Dai Ichi Waza
Technique #1
Ryote Tori
Two-Handed Grab: Steps 1 & 2

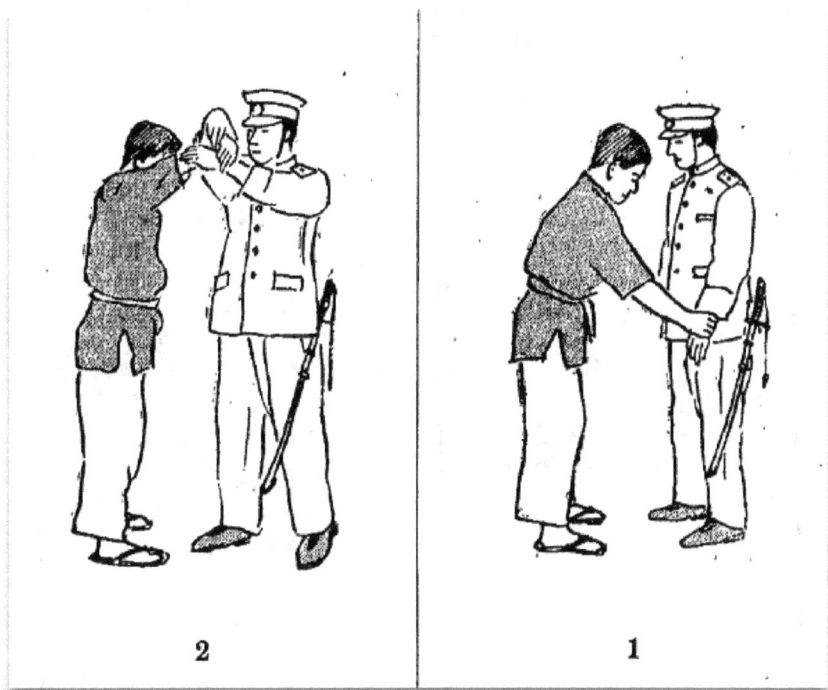

2   1

The attacker approaches you from the front and seizes your left hand with his right hand.[3] You respond by using the Freeing Your Hand motion introduced in the previous section.

As you do this, step forward with your right foot so you are standing just in front of the attacker's right foot. (This is shown in Illustration 2.) Wrap your right hand over the back of his left hand and grip his finger bones.[4] Then twist his wrist around and you have control of his hand.

---

[3] The text says, "Allow the attacker to seize your hand with both hands." however the illustration shows a one-handed grab.

[4] *Yubikotsu* 指骨 Finger bones. Probably just referring to gripping the fingers.

手

4

3

相手を引倒すと同時に左膝で上膊部を制して右手を背に廻し素早く捕縄を掛ける

上図の如く手首を逆に充分捻ぢ上げ右前隅へ引倒す

一四

Dai Ichi Waza
Technique #1
Ryote Tori
Two-Handed Grab: Steps 3 & 4

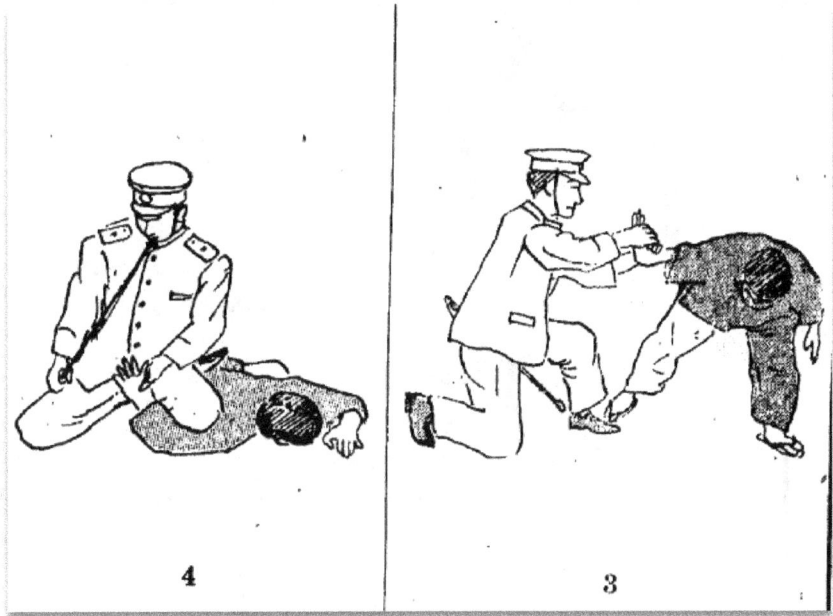

4

3

As Illustration 3 shows, reverse the attacker's wrist upward until he falls on his front right corner. As you pull the attacker down, plant your left knee on top of the upper part of his right arm to control it. This is shown in Illustration 4.

Then twist his right hand behind his back before rapidly using your Hojo, police rope, to tie him up.

捕

6

5

完全に捕縄を掛け終り連行せんとする所

右手首に捕縄を掛けて之を制し更に捕縄を左肩より右脇下に廻し再び右手首に掛け然る後左手首を取り同じく捕縄を施す

一五

Dai Ichi Waza
Technique #1
Ryote Tori
Two-Handed Grab: Steps 5 & 6

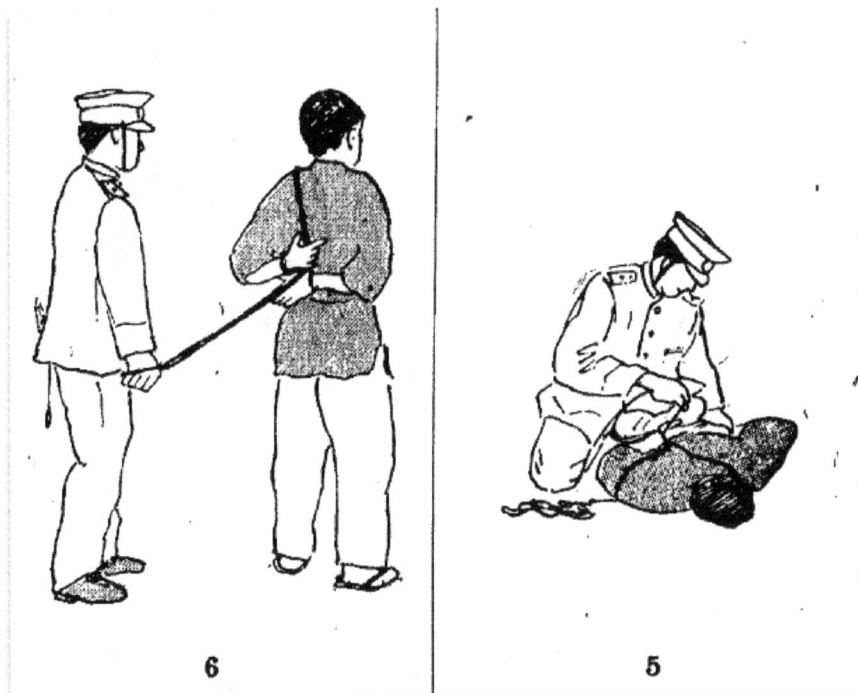

6 5

After tying off the Attacker's right wrist, thereby gaining control of it, pass the rope over his left shoulder and under his right armpit. Then wrap the rope around his right wrist again before bending his left arm behind his back and tying it above his right hand.

As shown in Illustration 6, after having completed your tie, escort the Attacker away.

第二技　　　小　　手　　返　　引

2

1

相手の右横脇に立ち寄り左手で相手
の右肘關節部を輕く攔み右手を以て
懐中を探り充分身構へたる姿勢

兇器其他を發見し又は逃走反抗等の
氣配を認めたるを以て素早く相手の
右手首を圖の如く取り右手を以て肘
關節部を強く上部へ捻ぢ廻し乍ら右
前隅へ引落す

一六

Dai Ni Waza
Technique #2
Kote Gaeshi Hiki Taoshi
Reverse the Wrist and Pull Down: Steps 1 & 2

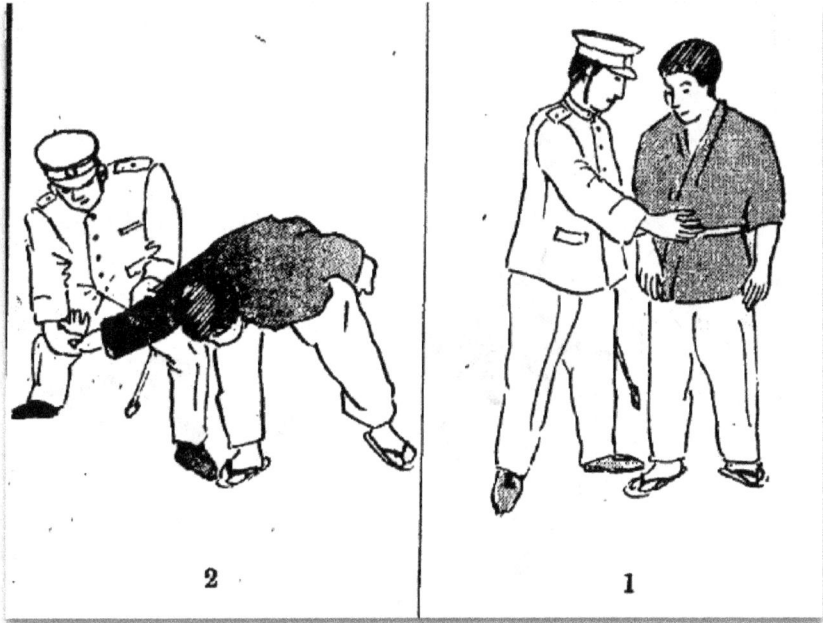

First, approach the suspect from his right side and block him. Gently take hold of his right elbow with your left hand. Use your right hand to search inside his breast pockets. Be sure your body is in a stable position, and you are on guard.

As the second illustration shows, you have discovered some sort of weapon, or you begin to suspect[5] the person you are interviewing will try to escape or resist. Rapidly take the suspect's right wrist as shown in the second illustration, while using your left hand to forcefully twist his right elbow up. As you are doing this step out to the right so you pull the suspect down onto his right front corner.

---

[5] *Keihai* 気配 is the feeling you know someone's state of mind or how they are about to act.

第三技

居　　　　　　　　落

1　　　　　　　　　3

後方より肩部を押し相手の兩手を出來得るだけ前方へ突出させる

引落しと同時に自分の左膝を以て相手の上膊部を制し充分右小手を搦め置き捕繩を掛ける

一七

Dai Ni Waza
Technique #2
Kote Gaeshi Hiki Taoshi
Reverse the Wrist and Pull Down: Step 3

As soon as you take the suspect to the ground, plant your left knee on the upper part of his right arm. Twist the suspect's right arm behind his back, being sure to apply sufficient pressure to his wrist so that you can safely tie him with your Hojo arresting rope. This is shown in the third illustration.

Dai San Waza
Technique #3
Idori
On the Ground: Step 1

As Illustration 1 shows, approach the suspect from the back and push his shoulders. This will force him forward so he will brace himself on the ground with both hands.

捕

3

2

突出すと同時に左手で頸部を制しつ
ゝ左足を相手の右脇下へ踏み出し乍
ら少しく相手の體を左に崩し突出し
たる右手を逆に背に廻す如く取り内
伏せにす

内伏せると同時に自分の左膝を以て
相手の上膊部を制し充分右小手を極
め置き捕縄を掛ける

一八

Dai San Waza
Technique #3
Idori
On the Ground: Steps 2 & 3

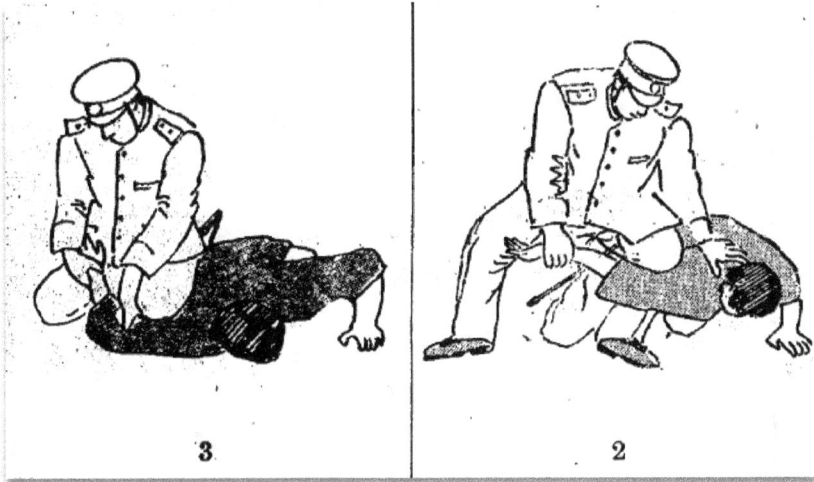

The moment the suspect braces himself on the ground with both hands, use your left hand to press on the back of his neck. This will serve to control him as you step forward with your left foot and press your knee into his right armpit, forcing the suspect sightly off balance and to his left. This is shown in Illustration 2.

Next, seize the wrist of his extended right arm and twist it behind his back, forcing him down onto his face. After forcing the suspect's face down, press your left knee into the back of his upper right arm. Make sure you have a tight lock on his right wrist before you tie him up with your police rope. This is shown in Illustration 3.

第四技

横

1

2

右足深く踏出す

り素早く潜り對手を抱へつゝ後方へ

横面を打たれんとしたる時右脇下よ

裸絞となす

し左手を相手の左肩上より廻し込み

同時に自分の左足を眞後の方へ踏出

一九

Dai Yon Waza
Technique #4
Yokouchi
Side Strike: Steps 1 & 2

The attacker tries to punch you in the side of your face with his right fist. Respond by rapidly ducking under his right armpit and wrapping him up with your arms. As you do this, take a big step forward with your right foot.

Next, immediately step directly behind the attacker with your left foot. As you do this, slip your left hand over his left shoulder and take Hadaka Jime, Naked Choke. This is shown in the second illustration.

打

4

3

裸絞めの儘體諸共に後方へ下り十分
に崩し右手を以て相手の右手首を内
側より逆に取る

逆に取りたる相手の右手を背に廻す
と同時に相手の前面より左膝で肘關
節を制し右膝を以て相手の頸部へ接
着せしめ支へ置く

二〇

Dai Yon Waza
Technique #4
Yokouchi
Side Strike: Steps 3 & 4

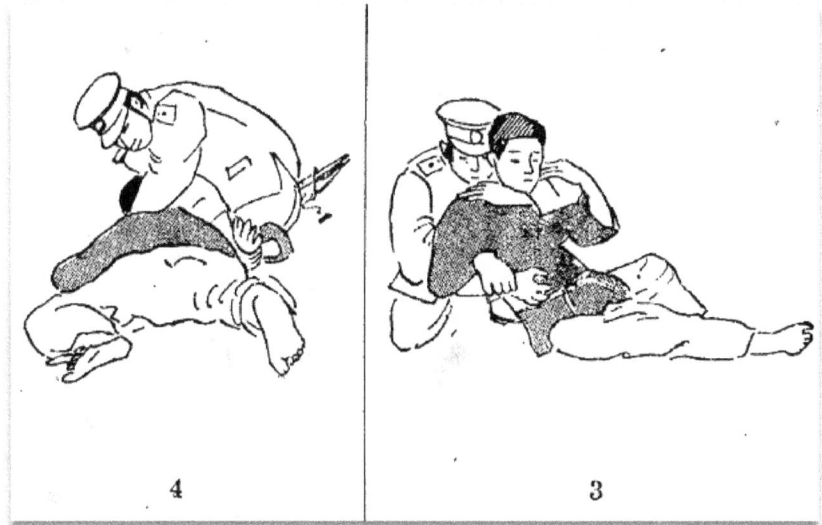

4	3

While maintaining Hadaka Jime, Naked Choke, drop back and down onto your right knee, taking the attacker with you. With your right hand you should grip his right wrist by threading your right hand under his armpit. This is shown in the third illustration.

With the attacker's right wrist in a Gyaku, or joint lock, twist his arm behind his back and, at the same time, press your left knee onto the front of his right elbow. Finally, plant your right knee onto his neck, holding him securely.

5

上圖の如く相手の右手小手を制しつ
、素早く捕繩を掛ける

Dai Yon Waza
Technique #4
Yokouchi
Side Strike: Step 5

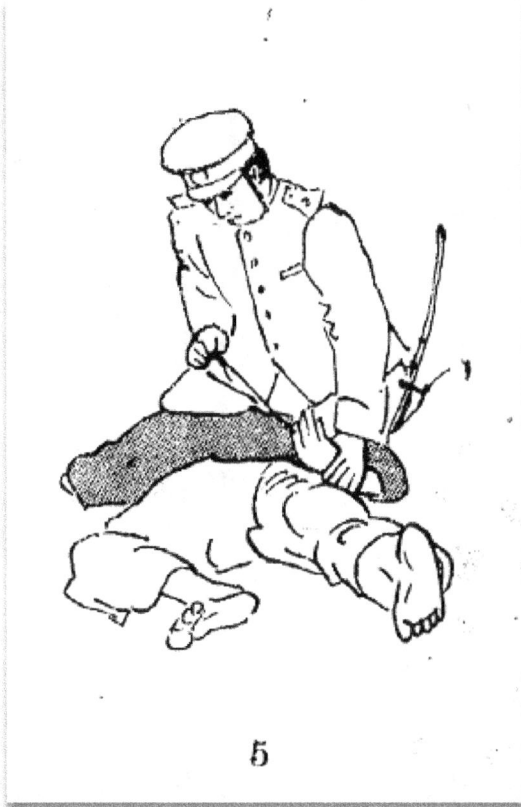

5

 While controlling the attacker's right wrist, rapidly tie him with your Hojo, police rope. This is shown in the illustration above.

持兇器者に對する場合

突掛、切下の技は持兇器者に對する場合であるが、我々警察官は時には太刀、短刀、洋刀、出刄庖丁、其の他の兇器を以て抵抗する不逞の徒に遭遇することも稀ではない。

そして吾々の先輩が貴い犠牲を拂ひ、或は得難い教訓を殘して呉れて居るのであるが、斯る場合に直面すると誰れしも興奮の餘り周章度を失するを保し難いのである。故に咄嗟の場合でも、自分に有利な體勢を整へ、之等の動作が無意識の中に出來る様に、平素鍛錬して置くことが肝要である。

兇器を持つて居る、ものに對して不用意に飛込んで行くことの無謀なるは勿論であるが、若し兇器を以て捕へた者に對し、警察官が已むなく之に無手で行く場合であるが、それは無謀かも知れぬが、然しそれかと云つて躊躇することは禁物である。相手の動きをぐつと睨み付け、そして突いて來るか、或は打ち下ろして來る時を利用して飛び込んで取押へる方法として、玆に突掛、切下の技を示したのであるが、能く之を翫味し實際の場合に役立つ様心掛くべきである。

How to Deal With Armed Suspects

This next section will introduce techniques to deal with a sudden stab, cut from above or other attack with an evil weapon. It is not uncommon for police officer to have to face a violent scoundrel determined to resist and armed with a long sword, short sword, Western-style knife, kitchen knife or other weapon.

Many of the following techniques we have inherited from the lessons learned due to the sacrifice of the honored officers that served before us, some of whom lost their lives. Other officers survived, but learned hard lessons. Clearly anyone who is faced with an extreme situation is aware of how it is difficult to maintain control in such confusing conditions. Thus, you need to be able to position your body in an advantageous stance at a moment's notice. However, to be able to position yourself without conscious thought requires that you conduct intensive training.

It goes without saying that to leap in and attack a person armed with a weapon is completely reckless, however there will be situations were an unarmed police officer will have no choice but to do so in order to arrest an armed suspect. While this may seem like a reckless act, you cannot hesitate in such a situation. To succeed, you must carefully observe your opponent's movements and, in the moment he attacks with a stab or cut from above, leap in, grab hold of him and force him to submit.

This next section will explain how to avoid *Tsuki-Kake* 突掛, stabbing attacks, as well as *Kiri-Orishi* 切下 downward cuts. Understand that if you pay particular attention to the details of these techniques they will be of great use if you find yourself in such a situation.

1

兇器を以て咽喉に腹部又は水月を突
かれんとしたる場合は素早く自分の
右足を後隅へ引き身構へて突きたる
手を上部より左手で受流す、

第五技

Dai Go Waza
Technique #5
Tsukikake
Defending Against a Stab: Step 1

The attacker is armed with a weapon and suddenly stabs. He is aiming for your stomach or Suigetsu, the solar plexus. You respond by rapidly pulling your right foot back to your back right corner. As you shift your body out of the way use your left hand to sweep the hand holding the knife past you. This is called Uke Nagasu, making contact and flowing by.

突

3

2

相手を倒すと同時に手首を更に反對
に內側へ捻ぢ返し充分小手を極める

受流したる手首を素早く捆み兩手を
以て小手を逆に返す
此の時相手は自然後向に倒れる

Dai Go Waza
Technique #5
Tsukikake
Defending Against a Stab: Steps 2 & 3

After deflecting the attack past you, quickly seize his wrist with both hands and force his wrist around in a Gyaku, wrist lock. This will naturally cause the attacker to topple backwards.

As the third illustration shows, as soon as you topple the attacker, twist his wrist the opposite direction, to the inside. Be sure to put sufficient pressure on his wrist.

掛

5

4

小手を極めたる儘背に廻すと同時に
相手の頸部を左手を以て支へ乍ら廻
す如くして内伏にする

内伏せにすると同時に自分の左膝を
以て相手の上膊部を制し充分右小手
を極め置き捕縄を掛ける

二圖

Dai Go Waza
Technique #5
Tsukikake
Defending Against a Stab: Steps 4 & 5

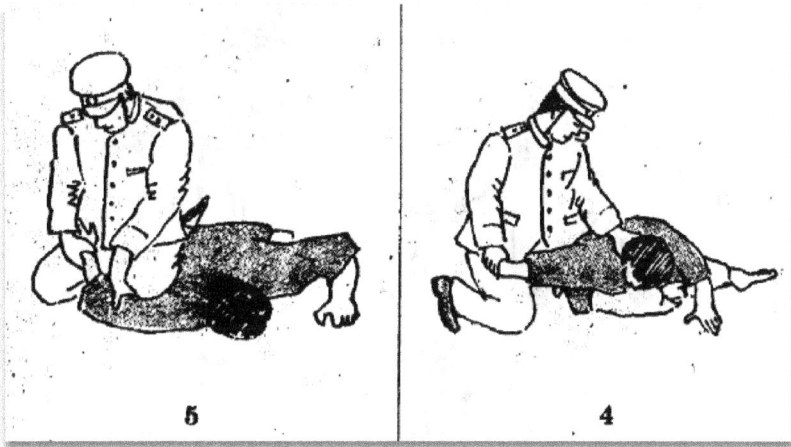

While maintaining pressure on the attacker's right wrist, force him to rotate off his back. Apply pressure to the back of the attacker's neck as you do this to help rotate him around until he is flat on his face.

As soon as you flatten the attacker face down, plant your left knee on the upper part of his right arm. This gives you control. Finally, apply sufficient pressure on the attacker's right wrist to allow you to use your police rope to tie him up.

第六技

切

2

1

眞向より切下げられたる時速かに自分の右足を後隅へ素早く引去り眞横となり右手を以て受流す

受流したる相手の手首を取ると同時に相手の左肩上より左手を以て襟を取り裸絞めの如く爲しつゝ制したる右腕を自分の下腹へ抱へ込み自護體となり抵抗不能の狀態に之を制す

二五

Dai Roku Waza
Technique #6
Kirioroshi
Defending Against a Downward Cut: Steps 1 & 2

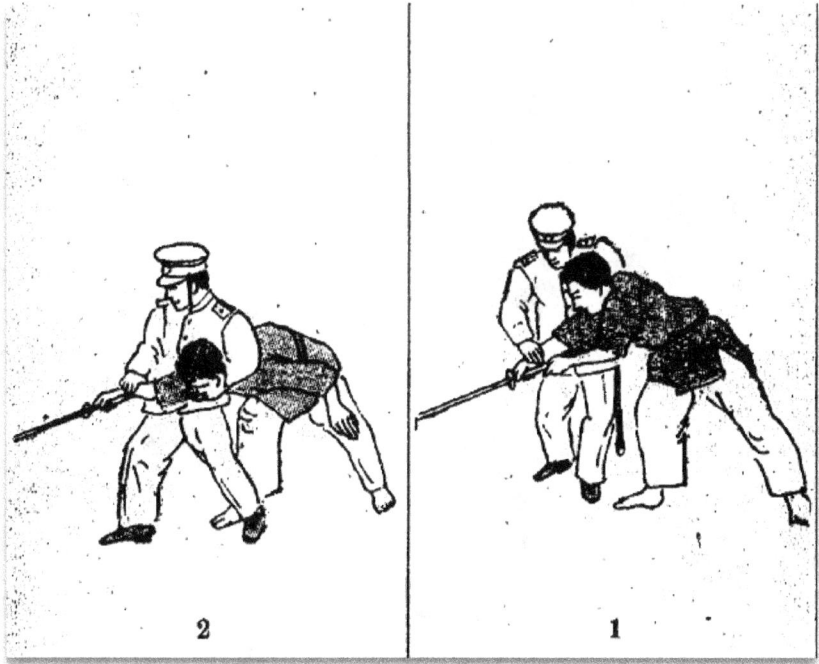

The attacker is standing directly in front of you and cuts down with his sword. As soon as you see him move, rapidly pull your right foot diagonally backward so that you end up directly beside him when he finishes his cut. Use your right hand to do an Uke Nagasu, making contact and forcing the attack to flow by you as you step.

As the second illustration shows, after passing the attacker's right hand, grip his right wrist with your right hand and hook your left arm over his left shoulder and seize his right collar. This will end up being Eri Jime, Collar Choke, allowing you to control the attacker. By pulling his right elbow into your lower abdomen, you can protect yourself and prevent the attacker from resisting.

下

4

3

取外したる相手の右上膊部へ自分の
左膝を以て制し更に小手を強く制し
つ丶捕縄を掛ける

抱へ込みたる儘相手へ寄り掛りて押
倒し右手首を制しつ丶自分の右足を
以て握りし兇器を取外す

二六

Dai Roku Waza
Technique #6
Kirioroshi
Defending Against a Downward Cut: Steps 3 & 4

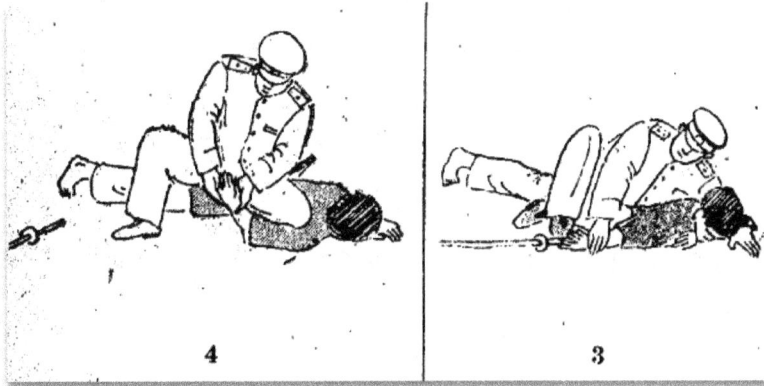

While maintaining your hold on the attacker, put your weight on him and force him to the ground. Once on the ground, control his right arm with your right hand and use your right foot to disarm him.

Having disarmed your attacker, next plant your left knee on his upper right arm. While keeping his right wrist locked tightly, tie him with your Hojo, police rope.

後 捕 り

逃走するのを後から追ひ掛けて捕へる場合であるが、御互に精魂の限りを盡して駆けて居る際には一寸した物に躓いたり、又後から少しの力で突かれたりすると前倒り易いものである。其處を利用して押へ込むで捕へる方法として此の遣り方が考へられたのであるが、之は居捕りの場合にも應用出來よう。

そして前倒すには如何にするかと云ふと、背中を前へ押し倒す様に突き、同時に足を拂ふ様にすれば尚更効果的であると思ふのである。

Ushiro Tori
Seizing From Behind

Police officers may have to chase after criminals and capture them. Since both you and the criminal will be running with every fiber of their being, if something catches your foot or pushes you even slightly from behind you will fall. Thus "Seizing From Behind" is based on this principle though it can also be used when you and the criminal are both standing.

As to how this technique will cause the suspect to topple, the answer is you will be shoving him from behind as if you are trying to push him over and simultaneously sweeping his leg. I feel this is a very effective method.

第七技

後

1

追跡して後から突き飛したるも倒
れざる時は背中から抱き付き乍ら對
手の股膝部を圖の如く支へ自分の左
足を進む方向へ深く踏出して相手を
押倒す

Dai Nana Waza
Technique #7
Ushiro Tori
Seizing From Behind: Step 1

1

If you catch up to a pursuing a suspect from behind, and despite leaping on to the fleeing suspects back, he doesn't fall, do the following. Use your left hand to push on his left leg, right where the thigh meets the knee. This is shown in the illustration above. Then take a big step forward with your left leg, which will cause the suspect to topple.

捕

2

3

押倒すと共に素早く背より馬乗りに
相手の內上膊部より圖の如く自分の
兩足を入れ起られんとするのを制す

充分制し乍ら相手の右手を內側より
逆に取り背へ廻し乍ら充分小手を制
しつ、左膝を上膊部に當て捕繩を掛
ける

二八

Dai Nana Waza
Technique #7
Ushiro Tori
Seizing From Behind: Steps 2 & 3

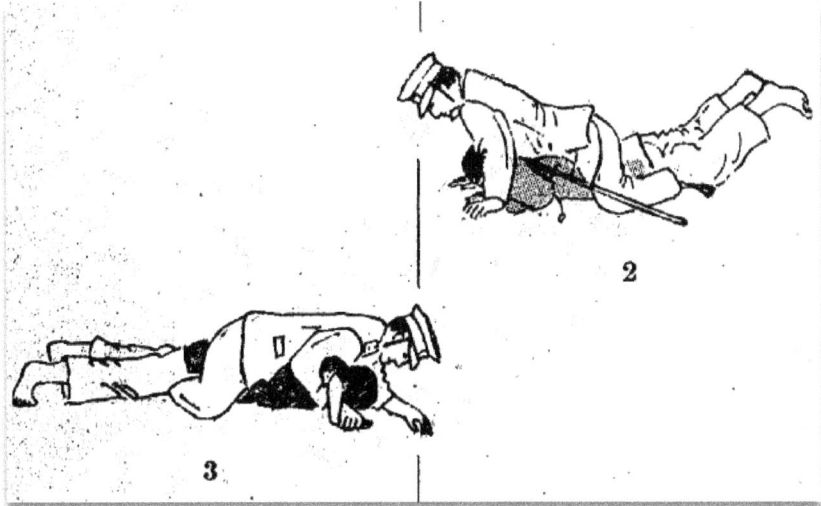

After you topple the suspect shift your weight forward, so you are Uma Nori, mounting him like a horse. As the second illustration shows, hook your feet under the upper part of the suspect's thighs. This will prevent him from rising, therefore giving you control.

While maintaining control of the suspect, reach under his right arm and seize his right wrist in a Gyaku, joint lock. Then, while maintaining a tight lock on his right wrist, twist his arm behind his back. Finally, plant your left knee on the back of his upper thigh and tie his hands off with your police rope.

End of Yokohama Manual

逮捕の要領

How to Arrest
Osaka
Arresting Techniques · Binding
Suspects Published 1941

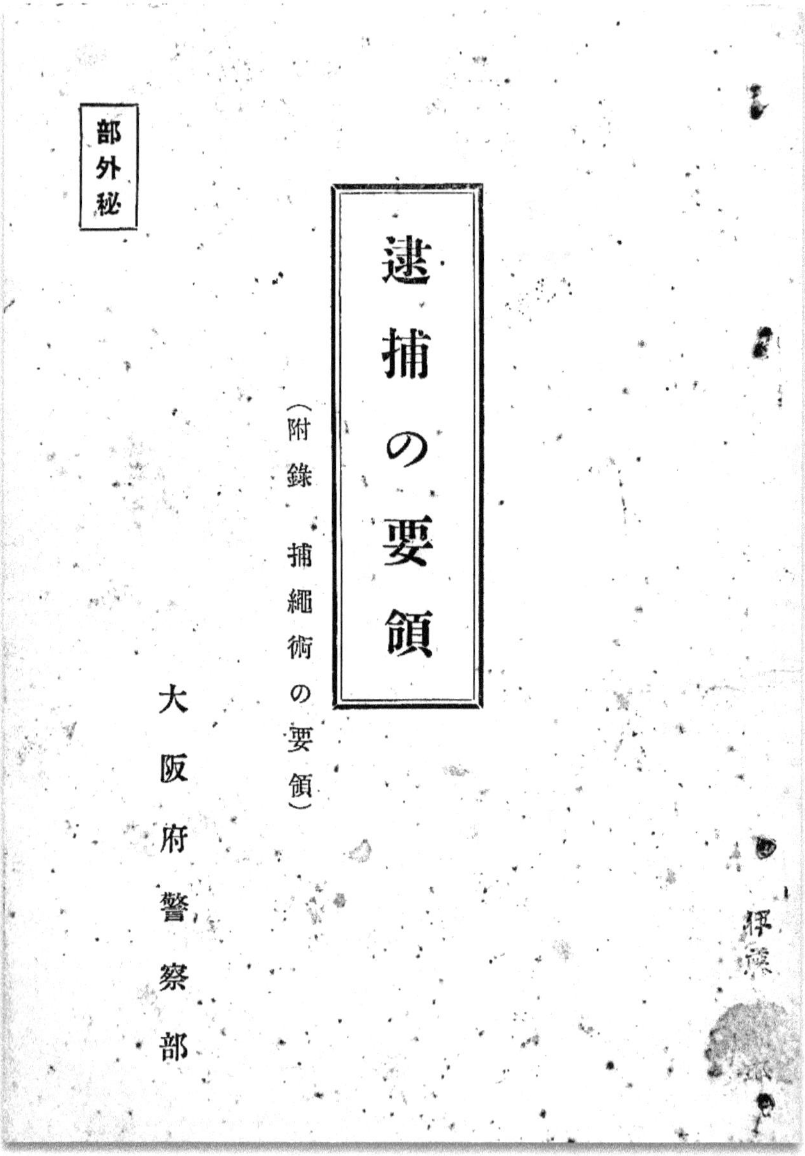

部外秘

逮捕の要領

（附録　捕繩術の要領）

大阪府警察部

Osaka Police Training Manual

Additional Material:
Outline of Hojo Jutsu, Binding With Rope Techniques

Not to be shared outside the police department

Osaka Police Department

◉逮捕の要領に就て

一、武術の合氣應用と其の特質

武術の合氣は警察官吏の實踐武技として應用し最も効果的なるものと認め今回之を應用した逮捕術に就て研究し一つの形として發表したのである。固より千姿萬態である實際の場合の總てを豫想して盡し得たものではないが平素絕へざる練習により突嗟の機に應じこの中のどれかでも應用に役立てる事が出來れば望外の幸であり其の目的の幾分を達したものと言ふべきである。合氣を警察の實踐武技として應用せんとするは其の特長とする所謂合氣を以て對手の機先を制し如何なる場合に於ても先に這入つて行つて而も身に寸鐵を帶びずして四肢を以て劍となすの妙用を發揮せんとするにあるのである。合氣は入り易く修得し難い術であり不斷の鍛錬を爲すに非ざれば到底所期の目的を達成する事は出來ない。即ち切磋琢磨の功を積まなくてはならぬ。而して修練の基本として手の握力腕力や關節や筋肉を強靱ならしむる爲め基本の形から這入つて行くのが捷徑である。之に依つて運足や體の變化も共に體得されて其の基礎が出來應用も容易になるのである。

二、誰何から逮捕迄の心構へ

The Essential Points of Arresting Suspects

1. The Particularities of Aiki[6] in Martial Arts How to Apply It

Incorporating the concept of Aiki from martial arts into the practical martial techniques used by police officers has proven to be very effective. It has therefore been incorporated into a system of Taiho Jutsu[7], arresting techniques, that we developed and presented here today.

In any encounter there are 1000 ways to start and 10,000 variations from that point, so it is impossible to prepare for each and every situation. Thus, the best way to prepare yourself is to train diligently on a daily basis. Then, if you were suddenly faced with a situation, you'll be surprised at how easily you are able to respond with whichever technique best suits the situation and affect the arrest.

The reason Aiki has been incorporated into the practical martial arts learned by police officers is because of the unique way it teaches learners to read the suspects intent and to stop his attack before he begins to move. By studying this system, no matter what situation you find yourself in you will be able to gain the initiative. Despite not being armed with so much as a Suntetsu,[8] Japanese brass knuckles, you will become able to move deftly, with your arms and legs responding in unison as if they are the blade of a sword.

---

[6] Aiki合気 means "joining spirit" or tuning yourself to the intent and actions of your adversary, being able to "read" what your opponent intends to do.

[7] Taiho Jutsu逮捕術 The martial art taught to police officers that was a combination of Jujutsu and Hojo Jutsu, rope binding.

[8] *Suntetsu*寸鉄 A type of concealed weapon. A metal rod with one or two finger-loops. The illustration below shows several Edo Era designs.

Incorporating Aiki into your martial arts is easy at first, but it is hard to master. Without extensive and continuous training, you will not reach a level that will allow you to perform your duty effectively. In other words, Sessa Takuma[9], training with other people in a friendly rivalry, is essential.

As for the fundamentals of training, you should focus on grip strength, arm strength and reducing the rigidity of joints and muscles. The fastest way to improve is by doing basic techniques. By doing this type of training you will learn how to who's your feet and body. Once you learn the fundamentals you will find you can apply them easily.

---

[9] Sessa Takuma 切磋琢磨 means cultivating your character by studying hard as well as mutual encouragement and friendly rivalry.

2. From Asking a Person's Identity to Arrest: Important Points

誰何から逮捕迄の心構へに付ては前回發表の「誰何の要領」に述べてあるが今回のものにはそれも含めてあり重複する嫌ひはあるが順序として一應簡單に述べて置く。

本來誰何は警察官の所謂第六感により對手の擧動不審なる場合にのみ之を行ふべきものであるがこの第六感たるや幾多の苦い經驗に依つて始めて得らるる處のものであつて何人にも容易に望み得るものではない。殊に犯罪者は努めて常人と異ならざる態度を裝ふを常とするを以て一見して直ちに容疑の有無を見分ける事は尚更困難で犯罪捜査に専從するものであつても容易な業ではない、從つて特に犯罪容疑なき事明白なる場合を除き服裝容疑の如何に拘はらず必ず一應誰何することは已むを得ない事とせなければならない。所が誰何を受くる通行人の多くは良民であつて眞の容疑者は仲々出會はないのが普通であるから何時しか心身に油斷を生じ偶々不良の徒輩に遭遇して不慮の兇害を受け或は重要犯人を逸脱せしむる等遺憾なる結果を招來するに至る様な場合が勘しとしない。固より良民に對する警察官の言語動作は極めて丁寧穩和なる事を要し如何なる場合にも初めから容疑者と目して之に對する様な假初な言動は許されない、又假令容疑者なりと雖も兇惡なる指名犯人であるとか抵抗の虞あるものの外は以下に示す様な方法を用ふべからざる事勿論なるも深夜通行中には兇惡な徒輩も亦勘くないのであるから此の點堅く念頭に置き常に左の如き氣構へを以てどんな場合にも不覺をとらぬ様而も誰何から逮捕の目的を完全に達し得る様周到な用意が必要である。

2. From Asking a Person's Identity to Arrest: Important Points

The previous volume, *Questioning Suspects* [10] contained an outline of asking a person's identity and while repeating this information again may seem redundant, I would like to give a brief overview as an introduction to this report.

Generally speaking, when questioning someone, a police officer needs to rely on what is known as his sixth sense. If an officer feels a person's actions are suspicious will he conducts an inquiry into the person's identity. However, developing this sixth sense requires going through a lot of difficult experiences and it is not something just anyone can start to develop.

A criminal is going to make an effort to disguise himself as a typical good citizen. Thus, when investigating it will be difficult to easily determine criminality in a person at a glance. Therefore, apart from rare cases where the situation is obvious, officers will have to question suspects no matter how they are dressed or how they appear.

However, most people passing by when questioned turn out to be good citizens, and as you might expect truly suspicious people never quite seems to materialize. Thus, you may allow your body and spirit to become careless. This means that when you do encounter and unsavory character, the unexpected situation may result in you being attacked or even killed. Further it could even invite the unconscionable situation whereupon you allow a serious criminal to escape. There are many examples of this.

Generally speaking, police officers should be patient and unfailingly polite when speaking with good citizens. No matter what the situation, an officer must not allow his initial questions to imply the person he is talking to is a suspect. For example, even if the officer is considering the possibility a person is a suspect, the person could be a dangerous wanted criminal and may resist arrest. This will mean you need to apply the techniques introduced in this book.

---

[10] 誰何の要領 I was unable to locate this book.

3. What to be Alert for When Questioning a Person

三、誰何の氣構へ

誰何せんとする相手方は常に

(一) 戒兇器の類を所持して居るかも知れない。

(二) 何時抵抗するかも知れない。

(三) 隙があれば逃走を企て或は容疑物件を抛棄するかも知れない。

(四) 虚偽の陳述をして警察官を誤魔化すかも知れない。

斯様に周到なる豫想の下に何時でも之に應ずるの心構へを以つて臨む事が必要である。而して警察官は原則として被誰何者の右側に接近し機先を制して相手方に抵抗の餘地を與へざる氣魄を示し常に其の氣配に注意し咄嗟の抵抗に備へつつ先づ第一に身體の檢査より始め戒兇器、贓物、犯罪用具、身體衣服の異狀等の發見に努め後適當なる訊問追窮に依りて之が答辯と其の態度に曖昧不審の點なきやを判斷すべきである。然るに從來の誰何の要領を見るに第一に住所氏名行先等形式的なる訊問より始め後身體檢査に移るものが多い。是は相手方に兇器を使用せしむるの準備と餘裕とを與へることとなり非常なる危險を伴ふ虞があるから充分改めなければならぬ。又一片の形式的訊問の後全然身體檢査を怠るものも見受けらるるが之は全く誰何の順序を誤るものと言ふべきである。

79

While this goes without saying, when patrolling at night it will not be uncommon for officers to encounter ruffians. As a police officer it is essential that you maintain the mindset described above. No matter what the situation you should not allow yourself to be surprised. Thus, to complete the chain of events from questioning to arrest requires you maintain awareness of your surroundings at all times.

3. What to be Alert for When Questioning a Person

Be aware that a person you are questioning could do any of the following:

1. The suspect could be in possession of some sort of dangerous weapon.
2. The suspect could become violent at any moment.
3. If an opportunity presents itself the suspect may try to flee or destroy evidence.
4. The suspect may try to give false statements in order to deceive the police officer.

Thus, as a police officer you should be prepared to react to any of the potential situations listed above. in principle when you approach a person you are intending to interview approach from the right side. Use the force of your presence to prevent him room to operate this will blunt any initial move he tries to make. Pay particular attention to the suspect's Keihai,[11] intent, in case he suddenly begins to resist

---

[11] Kehai 気配 is the sense of what a person is going to do. For example, feeling that a person is about to attack or about to run.

基本技 *Kihon Waza*
Basic Techniques

基本技

2

1

基本技は本要領を修練する上に基礎となるものであり足の運び即ち運足法と兼ねて腕力、握力を養ふ爲めにやるものであり最も重要なものであるから不断に練習が必要である。

先づ右手首をしつかり握らせる（少し熟練すれば兩手で握らせると尚効果的である）

手首から指先にグッと力を入れて右足を軸にして左足を後ろに引きつゝとられた肘をさげて手首の方から握られた手首を放す樣に上に伸ばす。

これを練習の初めに左右十回以上繰り返す。

基本抜 *Kihon Waza*
Basic Techniques

Illustration 1

Kihon Waza, Basic Techniques, are fundamental techniques to be trained in this program. It is essential to train these technique extensively as they develop your grip strength as well as show you how to move your feet. This is known as Unsokuho, How to Move the Feet. First the attacker grabs your wrist firmly. (As you progress in your training the attacker will grab with both hands. This is a very effective training method.)

Illustration 2

Put power in your hand from your wrist down to your fingertips. With all your weight on your right foot, pull your left foot back. As you step back lower your elbow as you extend your wrist up in line with the attacker's wrist. This will free yourself from his grip.

Initially, you should practice this technique ten times on your right side and then ten times on your left.

4

3

右足を踏み込むと同時に(2)と同様力をこめて伸ばす。

（之も練習の初めに右左十回以上繰返す）

同じく右手を握らせる

（この時握る方は對手が踏み込み易い様に左足を少しく斜に引くこと、同じく兩手で握ると効果的である）

Illustration 3

This version starts out the same.

(Respond by stepping back diagonally with your left foot. This will make it easier for you to advance toward your opponent in the next step. As was mentioned before, this technique is also effective if the opponent grabs with two hands.)

Illustration 4

Step forward with you right foot and, at the same time, put power in your hand as was described in the second illustration.

(Initially, you should practice this technique ten times on your right side and then ten times on your left.)

85

第一技 *Dai Ichi Waza (Tekubi Gyaku Hikitaoshi)*
First Technique
(Wrist Lock Pull-down)

第一技（手首逆引倒）

2　　　　　　1

第一技は對手が立つて居る場合の誰何から逮捕に至る要領である。

誰何に際しての心構へは對手の右脇から體を開いて油斷なく近寄ること對手の右手を制し自分の右手は利かしておくといふことが絶對の要件である、對手の右前隅から油斷なく近寄つて對手の右手を自分の左手で順に握つて制しつゝ身體檢査をする。

身體檢査は懐中は勿論ポケット內膀間靴の間ダブルの袖口等に至る迄心ゆく迄檢査しなくてはならぬ。

身體檢査の結果對手が若し兇器を持つて居る事を發見し或は逃走反抗の氣配を認めた時は上圖の如く右手を添へて左手で持ちかへる。

この左手で持ちかへる時對手の右手の甲の手より逆にとることが肝要である。

第一技 *Dai Ichi Waza (Tekubi Gyaku Hikitaoshi)*
First Technique
(Wrist Lock Pull-down)

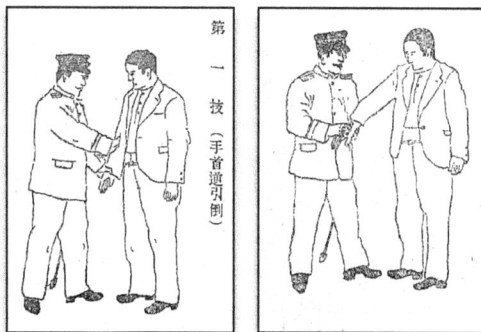

Illustration 1   *Illustration 2*

First Escape is used when you are standing and questioning a person and he tries to escape. The way you position yourself is very important. You should be standing facing the person diagonally in front of his right side. As you move in to control the suspect's right hand, you must maintain your awareness. It is absolutely essential that your right hand remain free to move if necessary.

Approach diagonally towards your opponent's right corner[12] then take hold of his right hand with your left hand as you search his body with your right hand. When searching a person, in addition to checking obvious places like his Futokoro, breast pocket, also be sure to check in his pockets, crotch, shoes and sleeves. All these places need to be checked carefully.

If you find a dangerous weapon in the course of your search or it is clear from his Keihai that the suspect will resist or try and escape, seize the suspect's arm with your right hand as well. This is shown in the first illustration.

Then, as shown in Illustration 2, you will switch your grip. Your right hand moves down to hold the back of the suspect's right hand. This is a fundamental step for setting up a joint lock on the suspect's right wrist.

---

[12] This is imagining a box around a person and then giving directions based on front left, right and back left and right corners.

87

4

3

左手にて對手の右手甲の方から小指の側にか
け右手を添へて手首を逆に捻ち上げ對手の肩
の方向に突き上げる様にして充分制する。
之はこの儘でも連行出來るが然し次に示す
様に捕繩をかけるのである。

右足を後ろに引いて對手の右前に廻り右手を
放し其の手を手刀の様にして上膊部を制しな
がら對手の右前隅の方向に引き倒す。

Illustration 3   *Illustration 4*

Next, reach under his arm and across with your left hand and grip by the little finger of the suspect's right hand. Use both hands to twist the suspect's wrist inward as you raise it. By shoving his wrist towards him and up towards his shoulder, you will achieve control. You can escort the suspect away like this or you can do as shown in the following step and use Hojo, or rope binding, to secure him.

As Illustration 4 shows, pull your right foot back. This will force the suspect towards his front right corner. Release your grip with your right hand and with your hand shaped like a Shuto, knife hand, apply pressure to the back of his elbow. Then force him down diagonally to his right corner.

6

5

引倒して自分の右膝で對手の肩胛骨の部を押へて制し右手を背に廻して捕繩をかけそれを頸にかけて更に右手首にかけ一巻き巻いて左手をとつて右手の上にかさねて兩手一所に縛り充分制縛する。

繩は後頭部の方からかけること顔の方からかけると頸にかかつたり嚙みつかれたりする虞がある。

背に廻した手は充分引き上げてゆるまぬ様かけること。

右足を引いて對手の右前隅にしごく様に引き倒す。

Illustration 5   *Illustration 6*

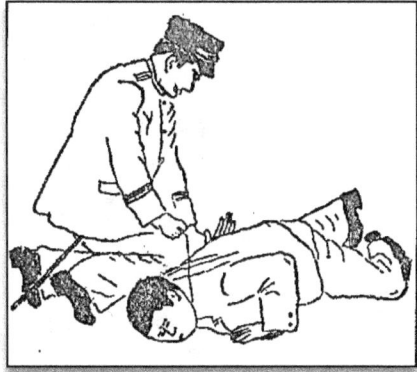

As illustration 5 shows, pull the suspect diagonally down towards his right shoulder.

As illustration 6 shows, after pulling the suspect down, control him by planting your right knee on his shoulder blade. Bring his right arm around to his back and loop your Hojo, police rope, around his wrist before threading it around his neck before bringing it back down to his right wrist. Wrap it around his wrist once before putting his left hand on top of his right and tying them together securely.

Be aware that if you start wrapping the rope from the back of his head, as it goes around the front of his face it is likely to go across his jaw or in his mouth.

Make sure you force the suspect's hands up his back high enough and ensure the rope isn't loose anywhere.

7

縛り終ると起して立たし連行する。

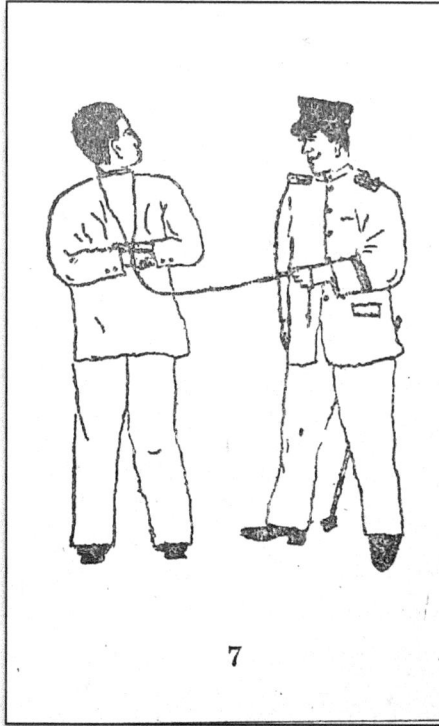

Illustration 7

After you finish tying the suspect, pull him to his feet and escort him away.

変化技 *Henka Waza (Dai Ichi Waza no Ni)*
(Mawari Komi Hiki Taoshi)
Variation of First Technique #2
(Rotate Around and Pull-down)

變化技 （第一技の二） （廻込引倒）

1

對手の右前隅から油斷なく近寄つて對手の右
手を自分の左手にて順に握つて制しつゝ身體
檢査をする。
身體檢査は懷中は勿論ポケット內胯間靴の
間等隈なく得心のゆく迄檢査しなくてはな
らない。

変化技 *Henka Waza (Dai Ichi Waza no Ni)*
(Mawari Komi Hiki Taoshi)
Variation of First Technique #2
(Rotate Around and Pull-down)

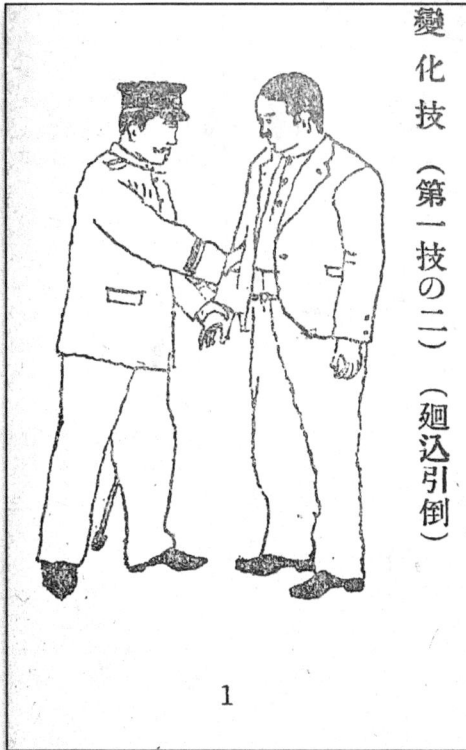

Illustration 1

Approach the suspect diagonally toward his right side. Take hold of his right wrist with your left hand and grip it to control him. Then use your right hand to search him.

When searching a person in addition to obvious places like his Futokoro, breast pocket, also be sure to check corner-to-corner in his pockets, crotch, shoes and sleeves. All these places need to be checked carefully.

95

3

2

對手が若し兇器を持つて居る事を發見したり
逃走反抗等の氣配を認めた時又は對手がとら
れまいとして手を引いた場合は上圖の如く右
手を添へて。

對手の手首を握りなるべくその手首に自分の
頭をつける様にして脇の下を潜つて後ろに廻
り其の手を逆に捻ち上げる。

Illustration 2   *Illustration 3*

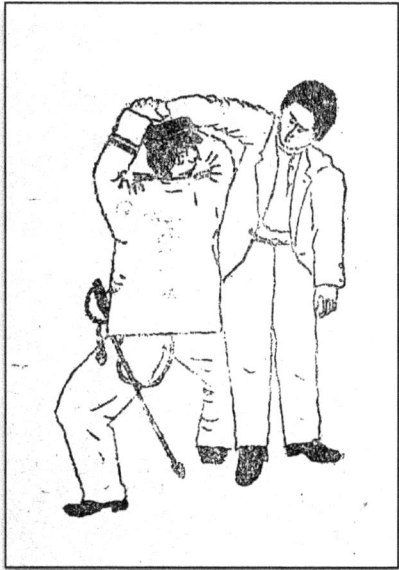

If you find a dangerous weapon in the course of your search or it is clear from his Keihai that the suspect will resist, try to escape, or try and yank his hand free, then join your right hand to your left. This is shown in the second illustration.

As illustration 3 shows, while holding his hand drop down low. You should be low enough that his wrist is touching your head. Then rotate counterclockwise under his armpit. This will twist his arm and force it up.

5

4

右手にて對手の右手の甲の方から小指の側にかけ右手を添へて手首を逆に捻ち上げ對手の肩の方向に突き上げる様にして充分制する。

之はこのまゝでも連行出來るが然し次のやうにして捕繩をかける。

右足を後ろに引いて對手の右前に廻り右手を放し其の手を手刀のやうにして上膊部を制しながら對手の右前隅の方向に引き倒す。

Illustration 4 *Illustration 5*

Next, reach under his arm and across with your left hand and grip by the little finger of the suspect's right hand. Use both hands to twist the suspect's wrist inward as you raise it. By shoving his wrist towards him and up towards his shoulder, you will achieve control.

You can escort the suspect away like this or you can do as shown in the following step and use Hojo, or rope binding, to secure him.

As illustration 4 shows, pull your right foot back. This will force the suspect towards his front right corner. Release your grip with your right hand and with your hand shaped like a Shuto, knife hand, apply pressure to the back of his elbow. Then force him down diagonally to his right corner.[13]

---

[13] These are the same illustrations and instructions as the previous technique.

7

6

縛り終ると起して立たし連行する。

引倒して自分の右膝で對手の肩胛骨の部を押
へて制し右手を背に廻して捕繩をかけそれを
頸にかけて更に右手首にかけ一卷き巻いて左
手をとつて右手の上に重ねて兩手一所に縛り
充分制縛する。

繩は後頭部の方からかけること顔の方から
かけると頸にかゝつたり嚙みつかれたりす
る虞がある、背に廻した手は充分引上げて
ゆるまぬ様かけること。

Illustration 6   *Illustration 7*

As illustration 6 shows, after pulling the suspect down, control him by planting your right knee on his shoulder blade. Bring his right arm around to his back and loop your Hojo, arresting rope around his wrist before threading it around his neck before bringing it back down to his right wrist. Wrap it around his wrist once before putting his left hand on top of his right and tying them together securely.

If you start wrapping the rope from the back of his head, as it goes around towards his face, the rope is likely to go across his jaw or in his mouth. Make sure you force the suspect's hands up his back sufficiently and ensure the rope isn't loose anywhere.

As illustration 7 shows, after you finish tying the suspect, pull him to his feet and escort him away.

第二技（手首取引落）*Daini Waza (Tekubi Torihiki Otoshi)*
Technique #2 (Wrist Take and Pull Down)

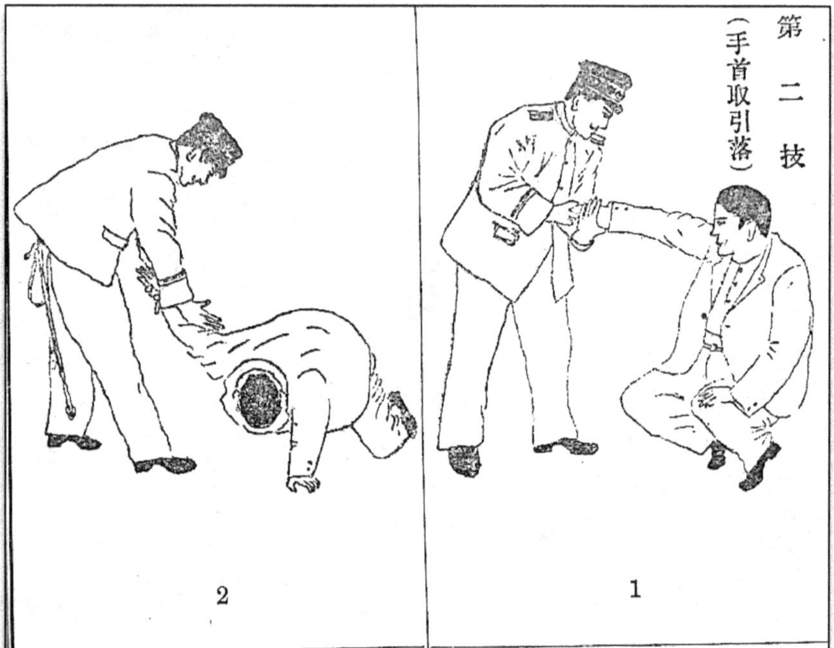

第二技
（手首取引落）

2　　　　　　　　1

相手が蹲んだり又は座つたりして居る場合は原則として一旦立たし第一技の如く誰何から逮捕迄の方法によるべきであるが立てと言つて立たぬ様なものは相當警戒を要するものであり其の儘制縛せねばならぬ場合も多い、例へば指名犯人の居る室へ踏み込む場合とか臨檢の時容疑者若は犯人と思料され而も反抗の氣配の見えた場合突嗟に座つた儘制縛するのがこの技である、先づ相手の右前隅から右手で對手の右手を取り左手で逆に持ちかへる。（第一技の手の持ち方と同様）

右手を放して手刀として對手の右上膊部を制しつ、對手の前方に廻り右前隅に引倒す。

102

第二技（手首取引落）*Daini Waza (Tekubi Torihiki Otoshi)*
Technique #2 (Wrist Take and Pull Down)

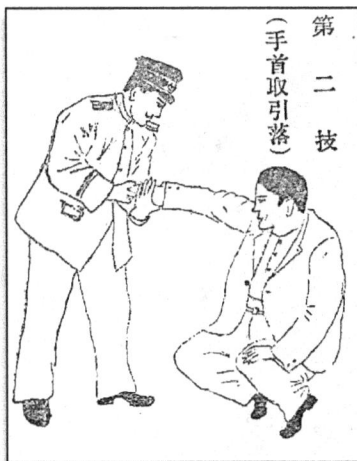

Illustration 1　　　　　　　　*Illustration 2*

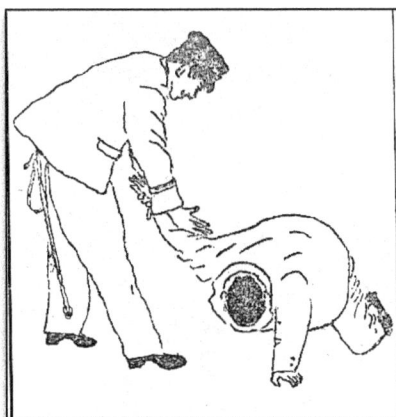

In principle, if the suspect is squatting on the ground or sitting, it is necessary to haul the suspect to a standing position before conducting the questioning shown in the first technique. However, if the suspect does not stand up when you order him to, you should be alert and on guard. It is often necessary to tie such a person up then and there.

For example, you may have stepped into the room of a criminal with a wanted notice out on him. Another possibility is while you are questioning a suspect, you realize he is a criminal and you sense that he may resist by suddenly sitting down. This technique shows how to restrain and tie up suspects in these situations.

First of all, as Illustration 1 shows, approach the suspect from his front right corner. Take hold of his right hand with your right hand and reach deep under his arm with your left to set up for a Gyaku, wrist lock. (This is the same way of holding the hand as shown in the first technique.)

As Illustration 2 shows, after twisting his wrist, release your right hand and, making a Shuto, knife hand, press it into the suspect's arm just above his elbow. Use this to control him and rotate him down diagonally toward his right corner.

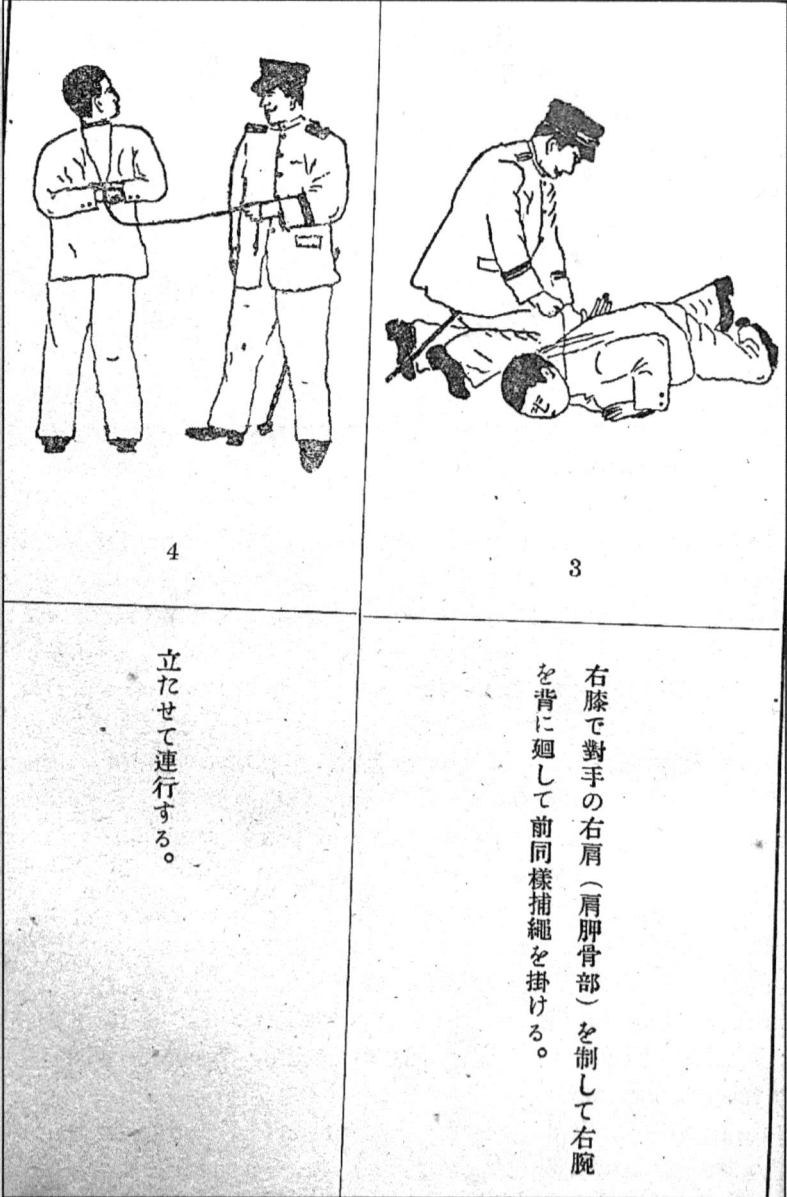

4

3

右膝で對手の右肩（肩胛骨部）を制して右腕を背に廻して前同様捕繩を掛ける。

立たせて連行する。

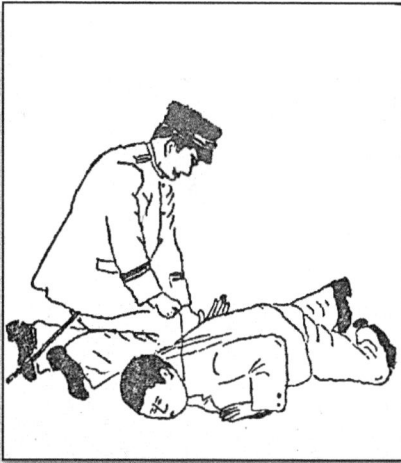

Illustration 3   *Illustration 4*

Illustration 3 shows how you control the suspect by pressing your right knee into the suspect's right shoulder (on the Kenko Kotsu 肩胛骨 shoulder blade.). You then pull his right arm behind his back and tie him up with rope as shown before.

Stand the suspect up and, as Illustration 4 shows, escort him away.

第二 變化技（二技ノ一）（持手廻引倒）

Henka Waza (Niwaza no Ichi)
Mochite Mawashi Hiki Taoshi

Variation Technique (Second technique, version 1)
Rotating the Hand You Are Gripping and Pulling Down

變化技（二技ノ一）
（持手廻引倒）

2

1

右手で持つて左手に持ちかへる暇のない時は
左手で其儘對手の右手をとつて內側に捻ちつ
、右手で腕關節を制しつ。
（熟練して來るとなるべく對手の手首を下か
ら取る程效果的である）

對手の右前隅に引倒す。

第二變化技（二技ノ一）（持手廻引倒）
Henka Waza (Niwaza no Ichi)
Mochite Mawashi Hiki Taoshi

Variation Technique (Second technique, version 1)
Rotating the Hand You Are Gripping and Pulling Down

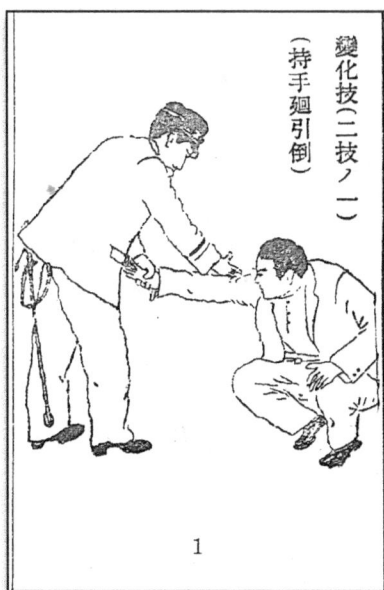

變化技（二技ノ一）
（持手廻引倒）

1

2

Illustration 1   *Illustration 2*

If, after seizing the suspect's right hand with your left hand, you don't have time to use your left hand to apply a wrist lock on the suspect, instead use your right hand to rotate the suspect's right arm clockwise. Do this by using your right hand[14] to press into and control his elbow joint.

(This technique requires a lot of practice but can be as effective as grabbing the opponent's wrist from below.)

As Illustration 2 shows, pull him down towards his right front corner.

---

[14] The illustration shows your right hand in a Shuto, knife hand, though the text does not mention this.

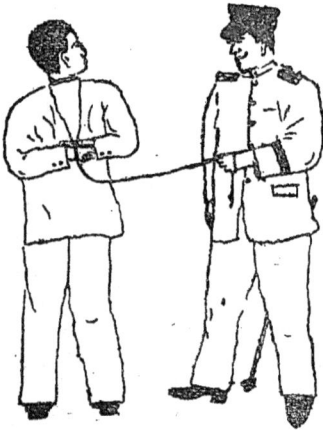

4

3

起たして連行する。

右手を背に廻して捕縄を掛け。

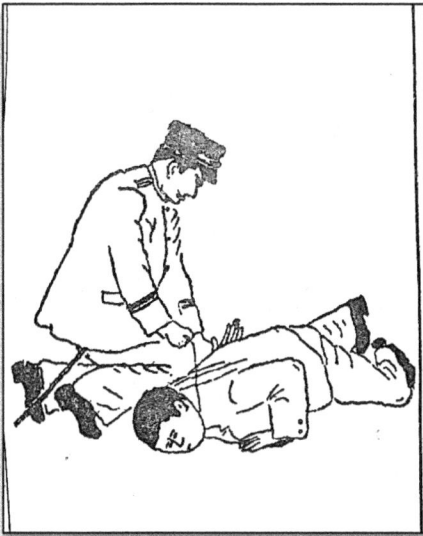

Illustration 3   *Illustration 4*

Twist the suspect's right arm around behind his back and tie it with your Hojo police rope. As Illustration 4 shows, pull the suspect to his feet and lead him away.

變化技（二技ノ二）（片手取引倒）

Henka Waza (Niwaza no Ni) Katate Tori Hiki Taoshi
Variation Technique (Second Technique, Version 2)
One-Handed Pull Down

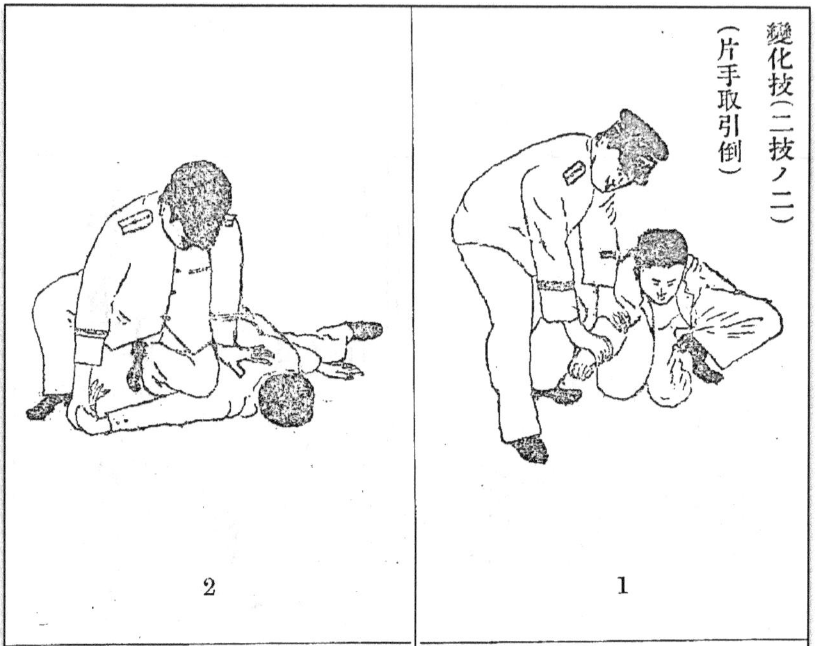

變化技（二技ノ二）
（片手取引倒）

2

1

右手で對手の右を取り外側に捻ぢつゝ、對手の右前隅に引出し乍ら突き倒す。

倒してから左膝で充分上膊部を制する、この時左手では對手の肩を押へ制すること。（對手の右手を出來るだけ前の方へ出して制すると効果的である）

變化技（二技ノ二）（片手取引倒）
Henka Waza (Niwaza no Ni)
Katate Tori Hiki Taoshi

Variation Technique (Second Technique, Version 2)
One-Handed Pull Down

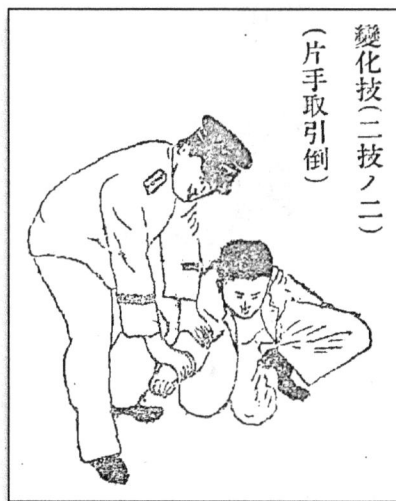

Illustration 1   *Illustration 2*

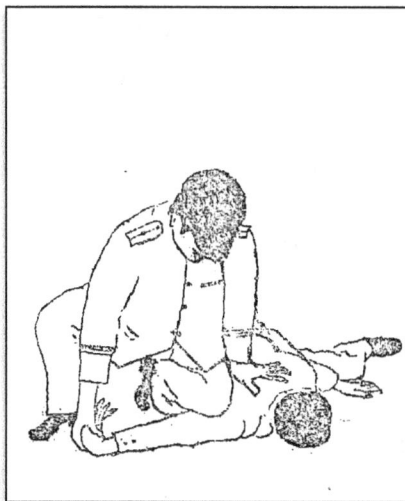

Take hold of the suspect's right arm with your right and twist it outward, pulling him towards his right front corner and shoving him into the ground.

Then, as Illustration 2 shows, after you take the suspect down, plant your left knee on his upper arm. Be sure to put enough weight on the suspect's shoulder to control him. You should also be controlling him with your left hand on his right shoulder.

(The further forward you push the suspect's right arm, the easier it becomes to control him.)

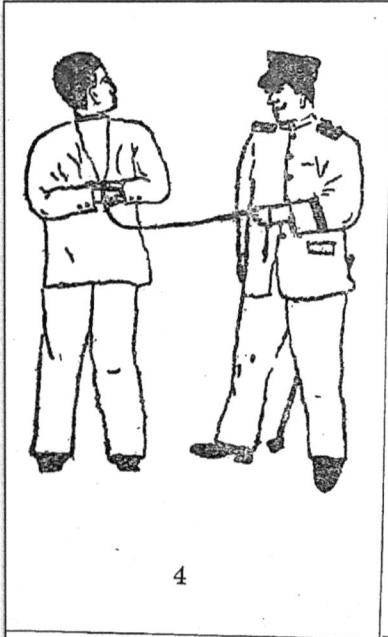

4

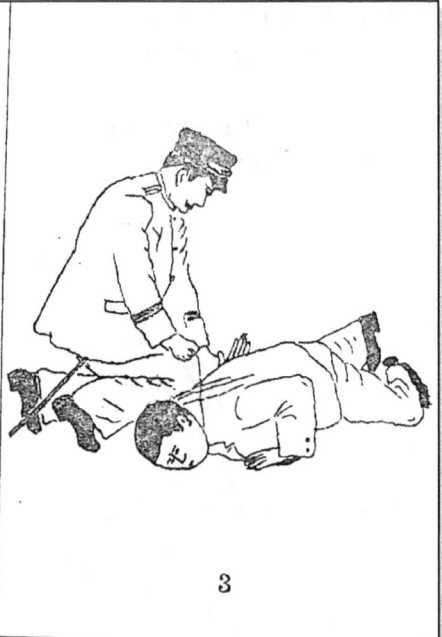

3

起たして連行する。

次に
頭の方へ廻つて對手の右手を背に廻し捕繩を
かけ。

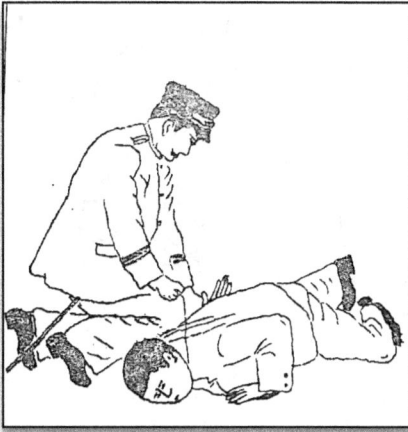

Illustration 3   *Illustration 4*

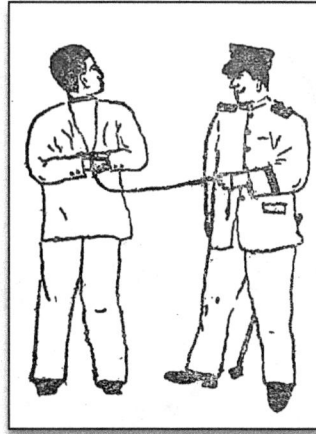

Next, wrap your rope around the suspect's neck as you twist his right arm around behind his back and tie it with your Hojo police rope. As Illustration 4 shows, pull the suspect to his feet and lead him away.

第三技（小手返捕） *Daisanwaza (Kote Gaeshi Tori)*
Technique #3
Wrist Reverse Capture

2

1

第 三 技
（小手返廻捕）

對手の右手を左手でとつて自分の右手を添へ
て對手を後方に仰向に倒す。

（左手を相手の右手の甲の方へかけ四指を對
手の拇指の方へかけ自分の左手の拇指を對
手の右手の甲へかける様にすること）

此の技は立つて居る者に應用することも出來
る。

對手の右手を一旦左に逆にして倒したのを圖
の如く左足膝外側部に當て、更に右へ逆にと
る。

（そうすると對手は自然に起き上らうとする）

114

第三技（小手返捕）*Daisanwaza (Kote Gaeshi Tori)*
Technique #3
Wrist Reverse Capture

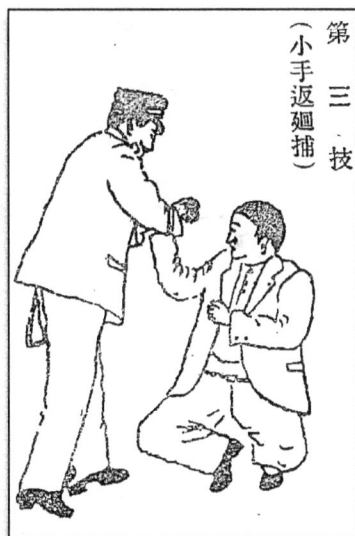

Illustration 1

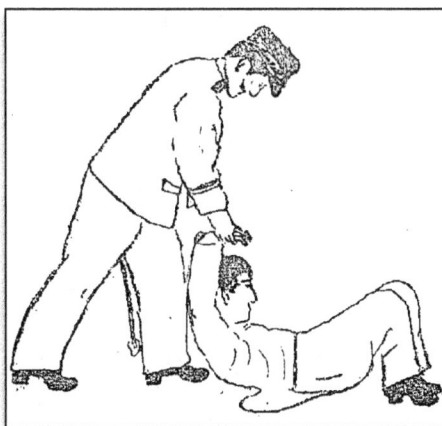

Illustration 2

Seize the suspect's right hand with your left hand, then join your right hand beside your left. Force the suspect's arm backwards so that he topples onto his back.

(Your left hand should be on the back of the suspect's right hand, with your four fingers gripping his thumb. The thumb of your left hand should be pressed into the back of the suspect's right hand.) This technique can also be used against a standing opponent.

As Illustration 2 shows, you first twist the suspect's wrist to the left causing him to fall. Then press the suspect's arm into the outside of your left knee before twisting him to the right.

(This will naturally cause the suspect to rise off the ground.)

4

3

素早く對手の頭の方に左から廻つて對手の頸を自分の左手で制しつ、圖の如く對手の頭部を股に挟み右手を背に廻して充分制する。

（此の時右手を左手に取りかへれば反對に右から廻つてもよい）

起き上る力を利用して圖の如く右手で對手の右腕を制しつ、前方に俯伏せにする様にして

（兩手で對手の手首を制して居るのを右手だけに持ちかへる）

116

Illustration 3   *Illustration 4*

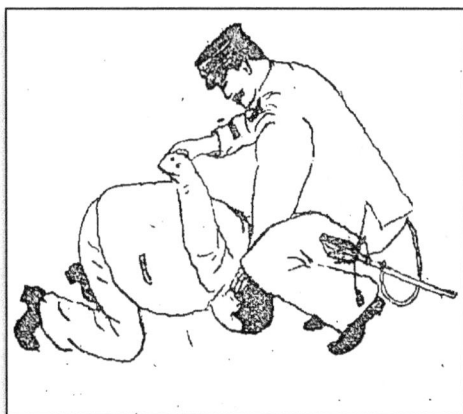

With your right hand to controlling the suspect's right arm, continue the momentum you created by forcing the suspect up off the ground to flip him face down.

(You have switched from controlling the suspect's wrist with both hands to controlling it just with your right hand.)

As Illustration 4 shows, you then rapidly move clockwise around the suspect so that you are in front of his head. Use your left hand to control his neck. As the illustration shows, you have the suspect's head between your thighs[15] and have twisted his right arm behind his back. You should have firm control of that arm.

(If you have taken hold of his left arm instead of his right, you would move the opposite direction, counterclockwise, after taking him down.)

---

[15] It's not clear if the author means to position the suspect's head between your thighs or to actually squeeze his head.

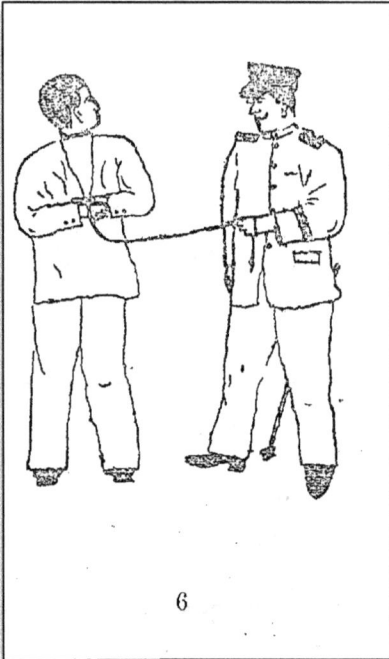

6

5

捕繩をかけ終ると起たして連行する。

そして右手に捕繩をかけてそれを左肩にかけ
充分引きあげて縛り、更に左手をとつて背に廻
し右手に重ねて縛り頸にかけて充分制縛する
（左肩に捕繩をかける時肩に深くかけること）

Illustration 5

Illustration 6

Then, as shown in Illustration 5, tie off the suspect's right hand before passing the rope over his left shoulder. Be sure to pull his right arm up his back sufficiently before twisting his left hand behind his back, placing it atop his right and finishing the tie. Ensure that the rope is placed around the neck securely, giving you control. (When wrapping the rope over the suspect's left shoulder, be sure it passes as close to his neck as possible.)

Illustration 6 shows the position after you have finished tying the rope and you are ready to lead the suspect away.

變化技（三技ノ一）（小手返引廻）

Henka Waza   (Sanwaza no Ichi)   (Kotegaeshi Hikimawashi)
Variation 1 of Technique #3
Reversing the Wrist and Pulling Around

變化技（三技ノ一）

（小手返引廻）

2

1

右手の逆を圖の如くとつて右膝に對手の右肘關節が當る様に一本の棒の如くして對手の肩先きに突込みつゝ逆に制する。

（此の時手首腕關節共に逆を利かして置く事が大切である）

前同様にして對手を後方に倒す。

變化技（三技ノ一）（小手返引廻）

Henka Waza　(Sanwaza no Ichi)　(Kotegaeshi Hikimawashi)
Variation 1 of Technique #3
Reversing the Wrist and Pulling Around

Illustration 1　　　　　*Illustration 2*

The movement in Illustration 1 is the same as in the previous technique. You topple the suspect backwards.

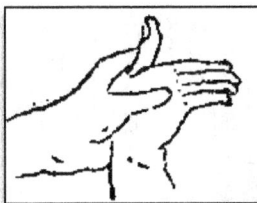

Take his right hand in a Gyaku, wrist lock, as shown in the inset drawing in the second illustration. Place the suspect's right elbow against your right knee. Force his arm straight as a pole and push down towards the suspect's shoulder, thereby using joint locks to control him.

(It is important that you have applied an effective Gyaku, joint lock, to both the suspect's wrist as well as his elbow.)

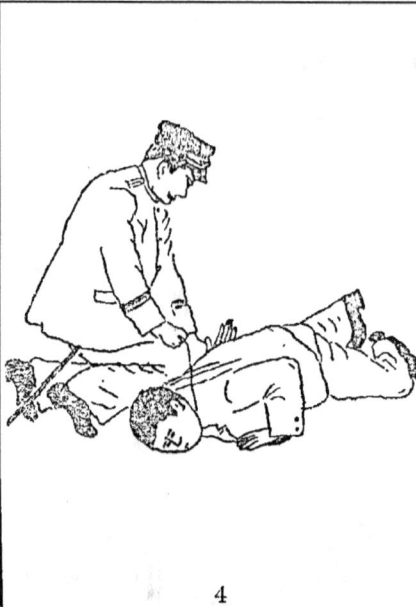

4

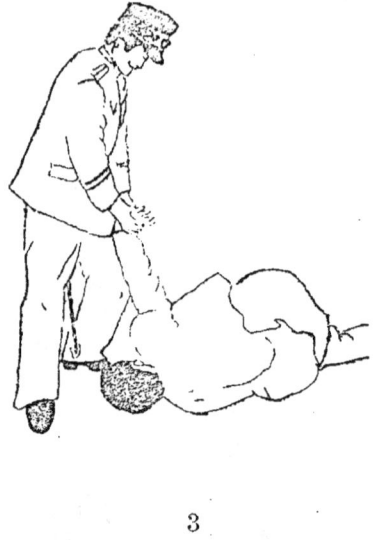

3

するど對手は右に起きれないから左側に起き
様どする其の時對手の肩を軸にして素早く對
手の左側へ廻つて。

（この時右手の逆をゆるめないこと）

右手を背に廻して捕縄をかける
この技は更に2から3に移る場合左の二つの
方法がある（これは又第五技にも應用出來る）
イ、2の如く右腕を逆に制しようとした時對
手がその手を引張つて伸ばさない時は手首
の逆を右手に持ちかへて曲げた腕關節を左
膝で押す様にすると同時に左手を添へて強
く腕關節を制して俯せにする。（小手返肘廻
し）
ロ、2から3に移る時對手が右手に力を入れ
て首を起さうとする様な時は手首の關節は
左手にて制し右手で腕關節を制しながら左
に廻る。（小手返し後ろ捕り）

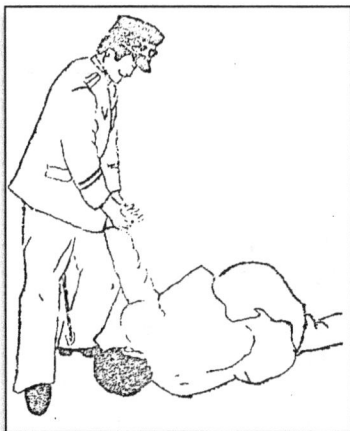

Illustration 3   *Illustration 4*

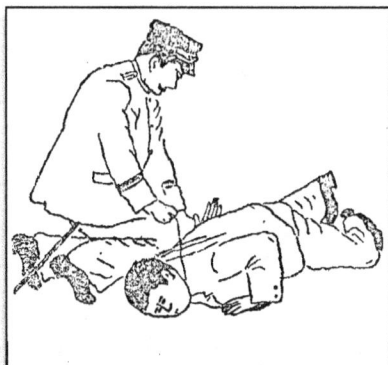

By locking the suspect's arm in this fashion, he cannot rise on his right side, so you will force the suspect to flip over onto his left. As Illustration 3 shows, while keeping his arm locked straight like the axle of a cart, quickly rotate him over on his left side.
(Ensure that you do not allow the joint lock on the suspect's right wrist to become loose.)

As illustration 4 shows, twist the suspect's right arm behind his back and tie him up.

When doing this technique there are two ways to transition from steps 2 to 3. (This also applies to technique #5)

Method 1: As shown in Illustration 2, you are trying to take control of the suspect by locking his right arm. He resists by pulling his arm in, preventing you from extending it. Reverse the way your right hand is holding the wrist lock and press the suspect's bent elbow on your left knee. At the same time, join your left hand to your right and force his elbow hard so that he topples face down. (This is known as Wrist Reverse Elbow Rotate.)

Method 2: If the suspect puts power in his right arm and tries to raise his neck when you are trying to transition from Illustration 2 to Illustration 3. Use your left hand to continue applying pressure to his wrist and take hold of his elbow with your right hand. Holding those two points rotate counterclockwise.
(This is called Reversing the Wrist and Pulling Back)

5

起だして連行する。

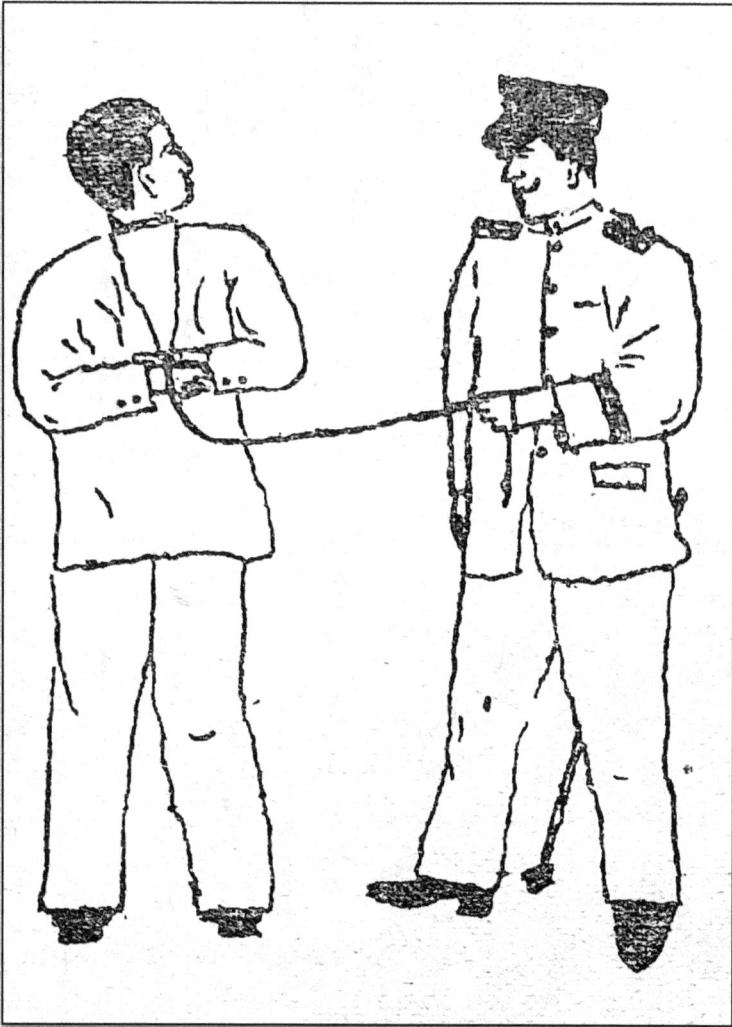

Illustration 5

Bring the suspect to his feet and escort him away.

Responding to Armed Suspects

◈ 持兇器者に對する場合

以下の技は持兇器者に對する場合であるが我々警察官は時には太刀、短刀、洋刀、出及庖丁其他の兇器を以て抵抗する不逞の徒に遭遇することも稀ではない。そして吾々の先輩が貴い犠牲を拂ひ或は得難い敎訓を殘して呉れて居るのであるが斯る場合に直面すると誰しも興奮の餘り平素の實力を發揮する事が出來ず或は其の措置を誤る事が多い。故に突嗟の場合にでも自分に有利な體勢を整へ次に示すやうな動作が無意識に出來る樣に平素鍛錬しておく事が肝要である。兇器を持つて居るものに對しては不用意に飛び込んで行く事が無謀であると共に兇器を以て構へたるものに對しては餘程心得のある者でも立向ふ事は難しい事であり之に無手で行く方法はないとまで言はれて居るがそれかと言つて躊躇することは禁物であり何か顏面に投げかけるなり誘をかけるなりして兎に角落付いて對手が突いて來る或は打ち下ろして來る時を利用して飛び込んで取押へる樣に心掛けねばならぬ。

Responding to Armed Suspects

The following techniques are for use when facing off against an armed suspect. Suspects will sometimes resist police officers and attack with long swords, short swords, western swords, kitchen knives or other such weapons. Encountering such lawless villains is not a rare event. Our forebearers, some of whom gave their precious lives, left us with some hard-won lessons about such situations.

Anyone placed in such a situation is liable to become excited and therefore unable to perform actions they are perfectly capable of in a normal situation. Mistakes in such situations are also frequent. Thus, when faced with a sudden situation you need to first position yourself advantageously, something you learn about when training. Then you must take clear action without having to first think about what to do. In order to be able to respond unconsciously in this manner it is essential that you train rigorously on a daily basis.

When facing off against an armed opponent, he may suddenly leap in with a reckless attack. At the same time simply facing off against an armed opponent can be a difficult situation even for a trained professional. Even if you are unarmed you cannot claim that there is "nothing you can do." You must engage the attacker in some way, without hesitation. That may involve throwing something in his face or employing some gambit to draw his attack. At any rate you need to remain calm when your attacker suddenly stabs at you or tries to swing his fist down at you, you have to be prepared to leap in and restrain the attacker.

第四技（突込み逆取）
Daiyon Waza (Tsukikomi Gyakutori)
Technique #4   Wrist Lock in Response to a Stab

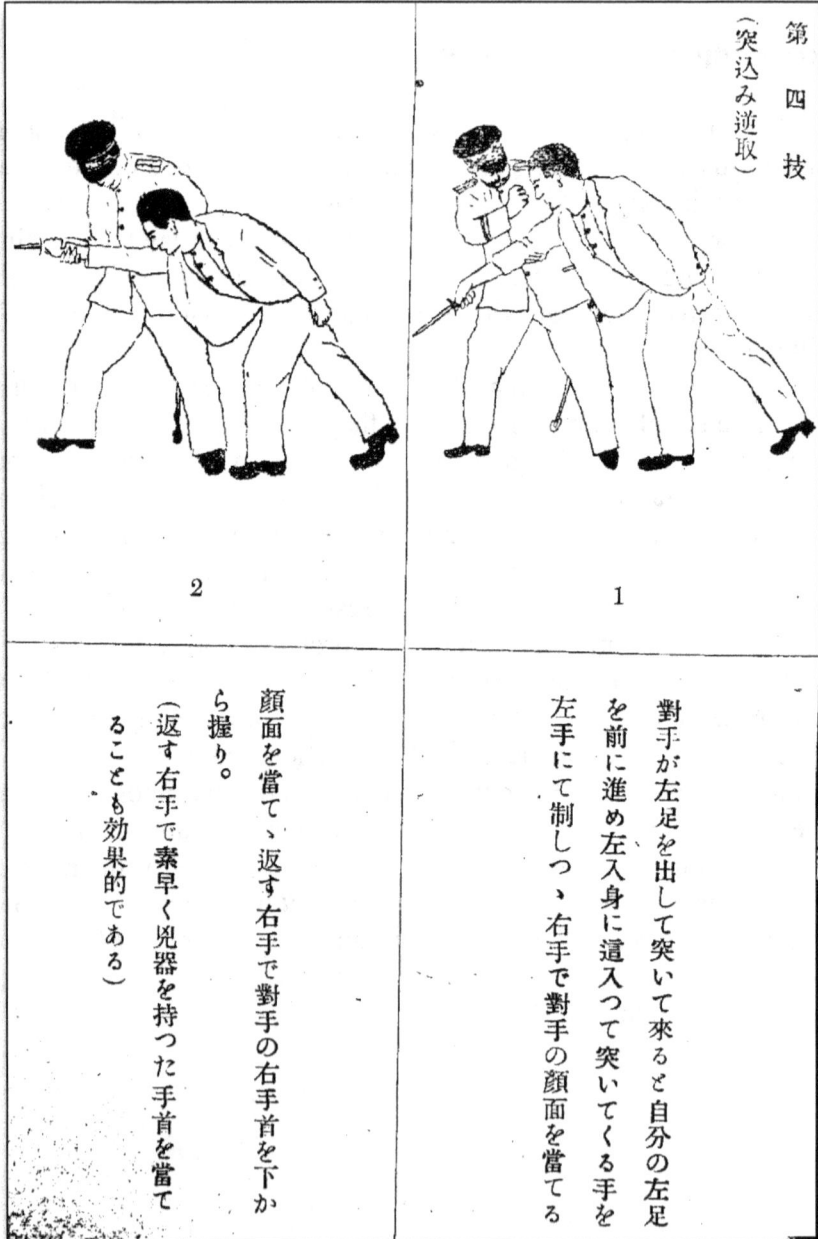

第四技（突込み逆取）
Daiyon Waza (Tsukikomi Gyakutori)
Technique #4
Wrist Lock in Response to a Stab

Illustration 1　　　　　*Illustration 2*

The suspect steps forward with his left foot and stabs. You respond by stepping forward with your left foot while rotating your body clockwise. Control the suspect's arm with your left hand and punch him in the face with your left fist.

As Illustration 2 shows, after striking the suspect in the face, drop your right hand back and seize his right wrist from below.
(Striking the wrist the suspect his holding his weapon in is also effective.)

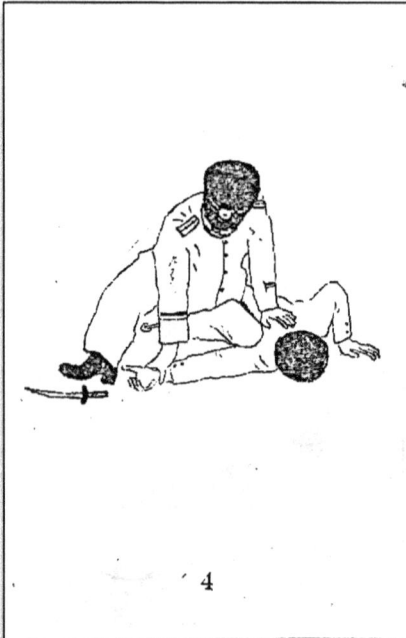

4

3

左脇にかい込んで腕關節を逆にとる。

そして其のまゝ下に落して腕を制し兇器をとる。

（對手の右手を出來る丈前の方へ突き出して制すること）

（圖の如く左膝と左手に注意）

Illustration 3

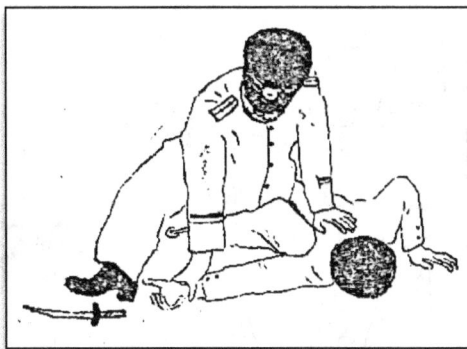

Illustration 4

Wrap your left arm over the suspect's arm so you are applying a Gyaku, joint lock, on his elbow, which is pressed against your side.

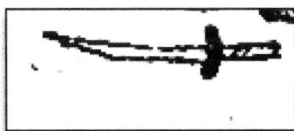

Next, as Illustration 4 shows, while keeping control of the suspect's arm, drop him to the ground and take his weapon.
(Control the suspect's right arm by extending it as far forward as you can.)

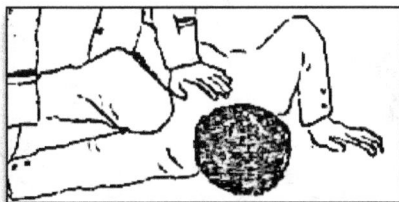

(Look closely at how your left knee and left hand are shown in the illustration.)

6

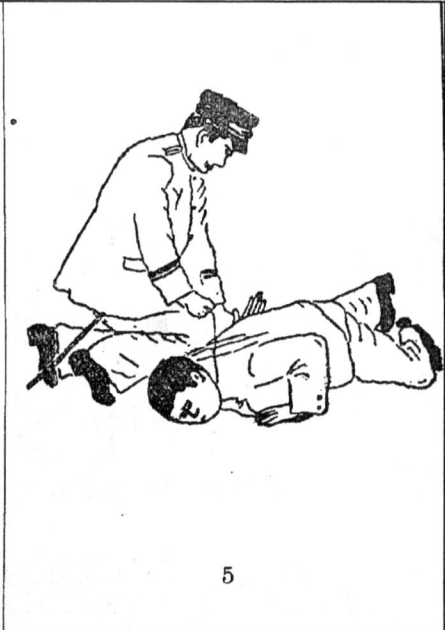

5

起たして連行する。

頭の方へ廻つて右手を背に廻し捕繩をかける

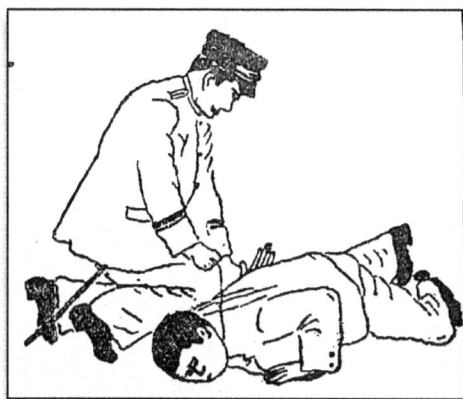

Illustration 5

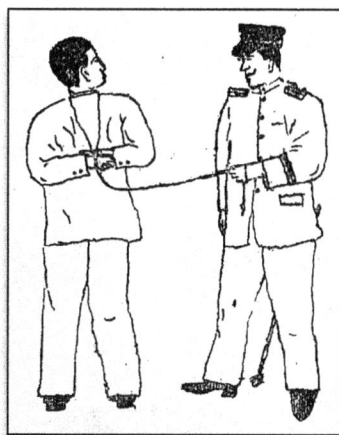

Illustration 6

As Illustration 5 shows, wrap the Hojo arresting rope around the suspect's neck as you twist his right arm behind his back.
Stand the suspect up and escort him away.

第五技（突込み小手返し）

Daigo Waza (Tsukikomi Kote Gaeshi)

Technique #5　Twisting the Wrist Back in Response to a Stab

第五技（突込小手返し）

1

對手が右足を出して突いてくると左足を軸にして體を右に開き左手で兇器を持った對手の右手首を制する。

（充分體を開いて對手を前に泳がせる様に右手を制すること）

2

そして素早く對手の右前隅に廻り右手を添へて對手を後ろ向きに倒す。

（對手が強く引張つた時は左手を添へ右足をそのまゝ踏み込んで同様に倒す）

第五技（突込み小手返し）

Daigo Waza (Tsukikomi Kote Gaeshi)
Technique #5
Twisting the Wrist Back in Response to a Stab

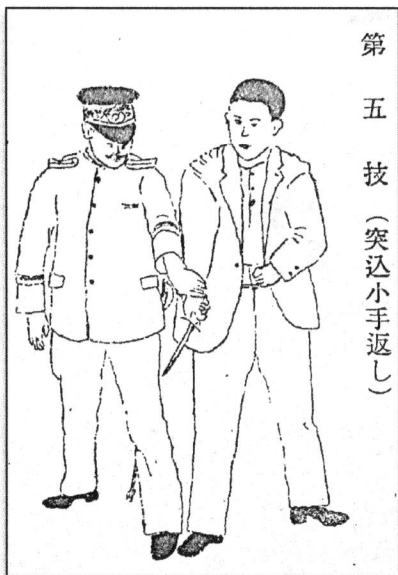

Illustration 1   *Illustration 2*

The suspect steps forward with his right foot and stabs. Respond by keeping your left foot in place and using it as a pivot as you rotate your body clockwise away from the stab. Control the suspect's right wrist, which is holding the weapon, with your left hand.
(It is important to rotate away from your attacker sufficiently. Control your attacker's right hand so it is out in front of him like he is swimming.)

As Illustration 2 shows, you rapidly rotate counterclockwise to the suspect's front right corner while joining your right hand to your left, then topple him backwards.
(If the suspect is strong and tries to resist by yanking his arm back, step in with your right foot and force him down and back in the same fashion as described above.)

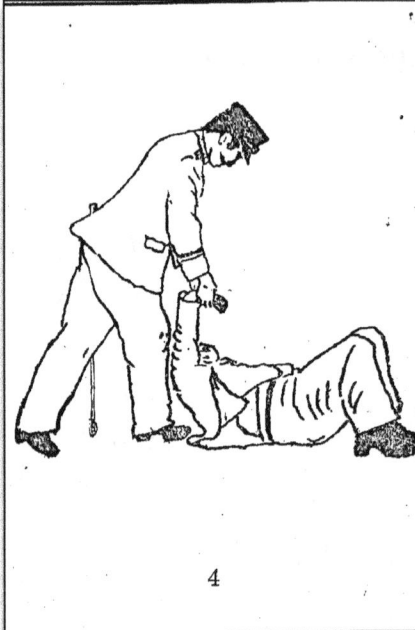

4

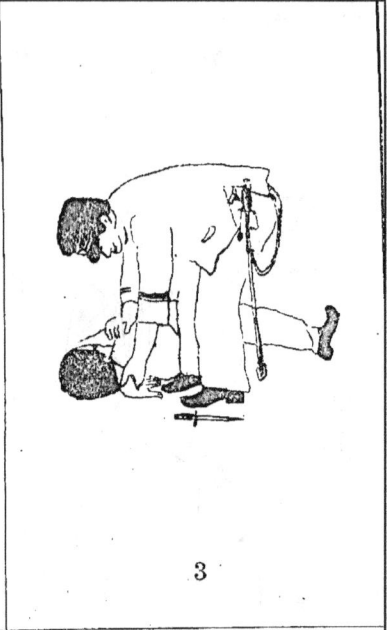

3

倒してから右手で對手の右關節を下に押しつ
け手首の逆を利かして兇器を足で取る。
（此の時對手が左手で抵抗しようとする時或
は相當頑強な對手と見れば右手で目つぶし
を當てると尚効果的である）
● 尚以下の制し方は第三技の變化技の何れを
應用してもよい。

對手の右手を一旦左に逆にして倒したのを圖
の如く左膝外側部に當て更に右へ逆にぢる。
（そうすると對手は自然に起き上らうとする）

136

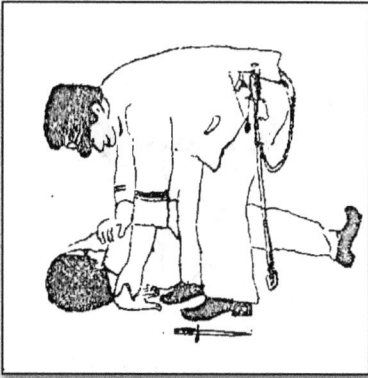

Illustration 3   *Illustration 4*

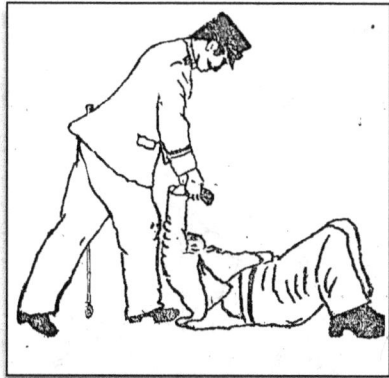

After you topple the suspect, use your right hand to control his right elbow by pushing down. Keeping pressure on the wrist lock you have on the suspect's right wrist, use your foot to remove his weapon.

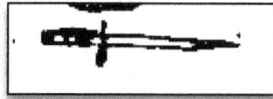

(If the suspect tries to resist with his left hand, or he demonstrates that he is extremely strong, use your right hand to strike with a Metsubushi, blinding strike to the eyes. This can be very effective.)

- Note that any of the Henka, variations, of technique #3 can be used to control the suspect from this point on.

Initially, you have twisted the suspect's wrist to the left in order to topple him, so next place his arm against the outside of your left knee. Then, after locking the suspect's arm, rotate his arm to the right.
(This action will naturally force the suspect to rise from the ground.)

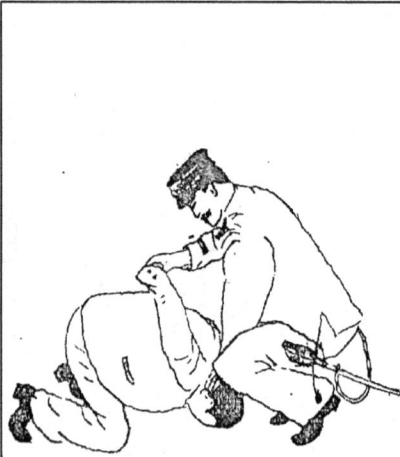

6

5

起き上る力を利用して圖の如く右手で對手の右腕を制しつゝ前方に俯伏せに倒す様にして

素早く對手の頭の方に左から廻つて對手の頸を自分の左手で制しつゝ圖の如く對手の頭部を股に挾み右手を背に廻して充分制する。
（此の時右手を左手に取りかへれば反對に右から廻つてもよい）

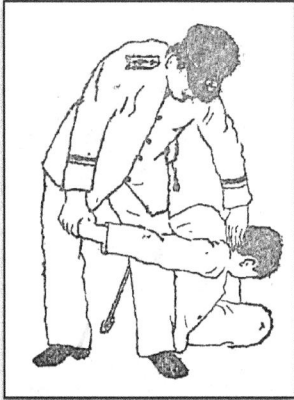

Illustration 5   *Illustration 6*

While controlling the suspect's right arm with your right hand, use the motion of the suspect rising to force him forward and down. This is shown in Illustration 5.

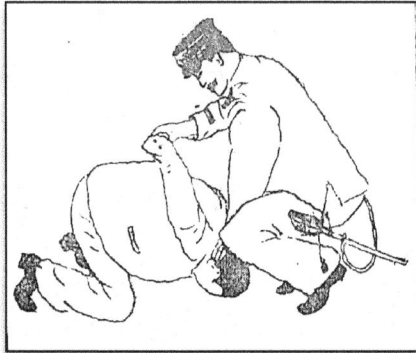

Next, as shown in Illustration 6, rotate around the suspect clockwise so you are in front of his head. Use your left hand to control his neck. Hold his head between your thighs as shown in the illustration. Then, rotate the suspect's right arm behind his back far enough so you have firm control.

(If you have taken hold of the suspect's left arm, then you would rotate around, counterclockwise, the opposite direction.)

8

7

そして右手に捕繩をかけて左肩にかけ充分引
きあげて縛り左手をとつて背に廻し右手に重
ねて更に頸にかけて充分制縛する。
（左肩に捕繩をかける時肩に深くかけること）

起たして連行する。

140

Illustration 7

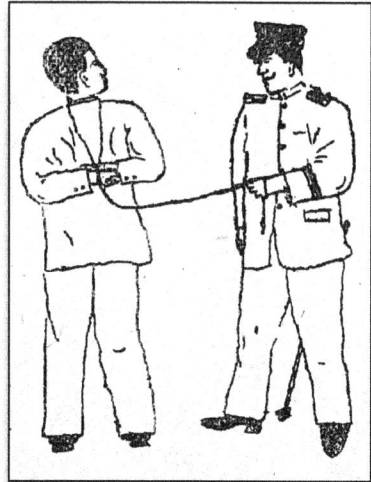

Illustration 8

Next, as shown in the seventh illustration, tie off his right hand with your rope. Then pass the rope over the suspect's left shoulder and pull so that his right hand is pulled up his back sufficiently. After that, bend his left arm behind his back and place it on top of his right. While ensuring there is appropriate tension on the neck, tie his hands together.

(When passing the rope over the suspect's left shoulder, be sure the rope is close to where the neck meets the shoulder.)

Finally, stand the suspect up and lead him away.

第六技（振上逆取）

Dairoku Waza (Furiage Gyaku Tori)
Technique #6.   Reverse Grab Against a Stab From Above

第 六 技

（振上逆取）

1

對手が逆手に振りかぶつて切りおろして來る
時は振りあげた瞬間素早く遣入り込んで右手
で斬りおろそうとする對手の右肘を制し右手
で脾腹を當てる。

2

當てた右手で直ちに對手の右手首を握り。

第六技（振上逆取）

Dairoku Waza (Furiage Gyaku Tori)
Technique #6
Reverse Grab Against a Stab From Above

Illustration 1   *Illustration 2*

The suspect has a knife in Sakate, a reverse grip, and has brought it up in the air. He is moving in, intending to stab down at you.

You should advance rapidly the moment the suspect begins to raise his knife. As his knife starts to swing down, control his right elbow with your left hand while punching him in the spleen[16] with your left fist.

As Illustration 2 shows, after striking with your right fist, seize the suspect's right wrist with your right hand.

---

[16] Hibara 脾腹 This can refer to the spleen or the side of the body.

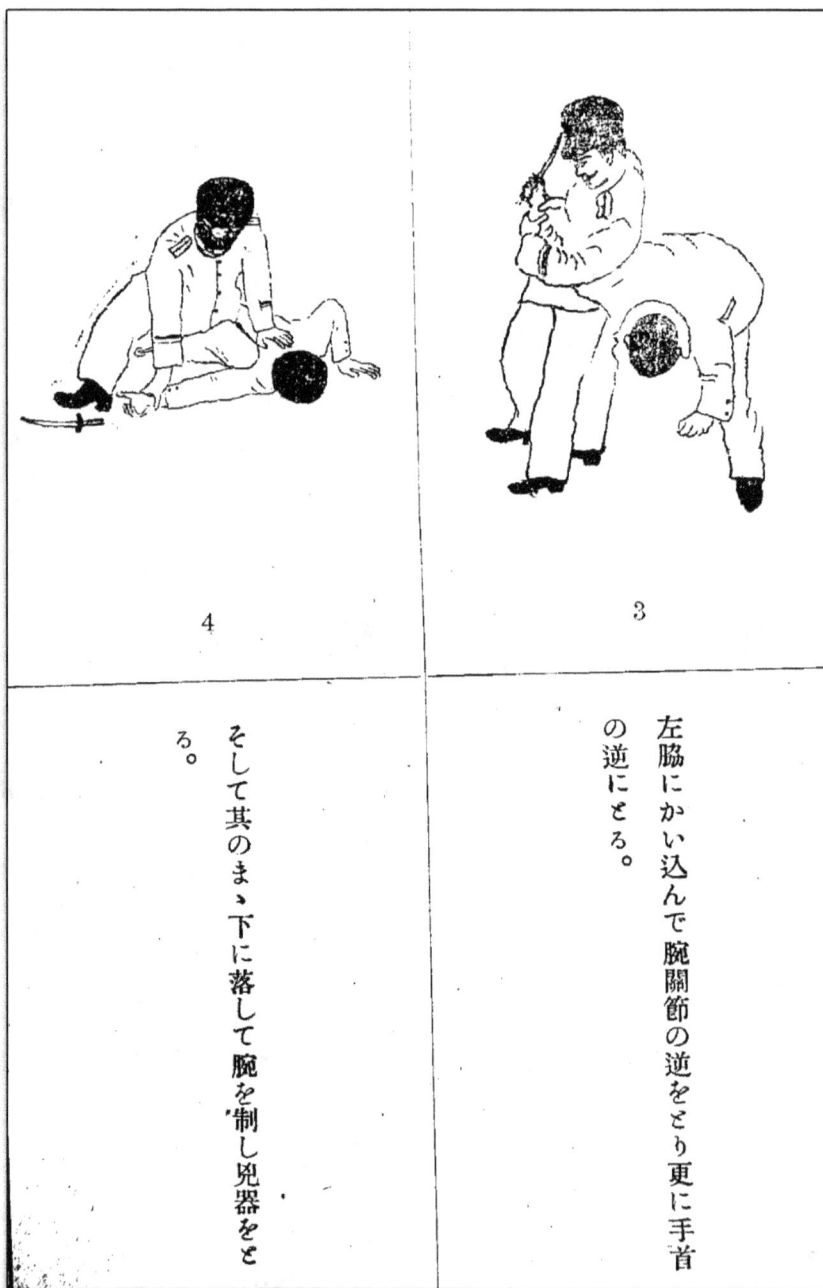

4

3

左脇にかい込んで腕關節の逆をとり更に手首の逆にとる。

そして其のまゝ下に落して腕を制し兇器をとる。

Illustration 3   *Illustration 4*

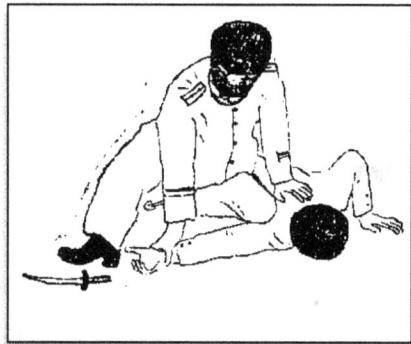

Next, wrap your left arm around the suspect's arm, so his arm is tucked under your armpit. You should be applying a Gyaku, joint lock, to the suspect's elbow as well as his right wrist.

As Illustration 4 shows, you then drop the suspect to the ground. Maintain control of his arm and remove his weapon.

6

5

起たして連行する。

頭の方へ廻つて右手を背に廻し捕縄をかけて

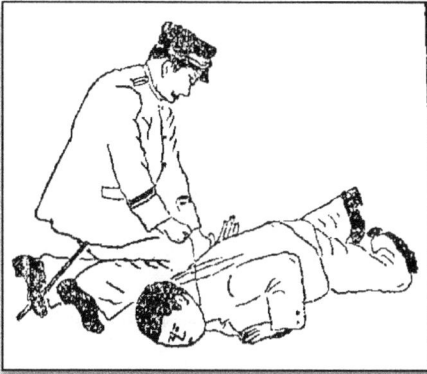

Illustration 5

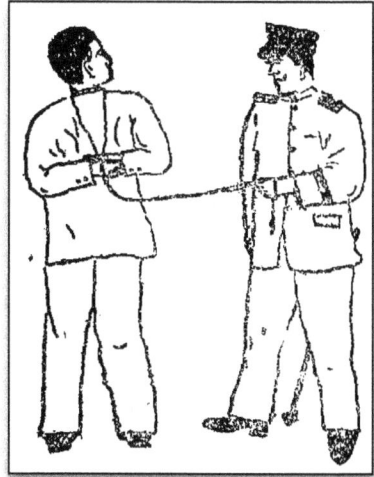

Illustration 6

Move around so you are by the suspect's head. Pull his right hand up behind his back and tie him up with your rope. Finally, bring the suspect to his feet and lead him away.

第七技（切下し小手返し）
Daishichi Waza (Kiri Oroshi Kote Gaeshi)
Technique #7
Reversing the Wrist Against an Opponent Cutting Down

第七技（切下し小手返し）

2

1

切り下して來たのを左足を軸にして體を右に
開き空を打たし對手の體が崩れた瞬間左手に
て手の右手首を握り右手を添へて。
（右手を添へる時必ず柄の所へ右手の指がか
ゝつて居ること）

圖の如く後ろに倒す。

第七技（切下し小手返し）
Daishichi Waza (Kiri Oroshi Kote Gaeshi)
Technique #7
Reversing the Wrist Against an Opponent Cutting Down

Illustration 1   *Illustration 2*

The suspect cuts down at you with his sword. You respond by putting your weight on your left foot and rotating your body clockwise, using your left foot as an axis, causing the suspect to cut only air. The moment he loses his balance, seize his right wrist with your left hand. Then join your right hand beside it.

(When joining your right hand beside your left, be sure the fingers of your right hand are hooked around the Tsuka, handle, of the sword.)

Next, as shown in Illustration 2, topple the opponent backwards.

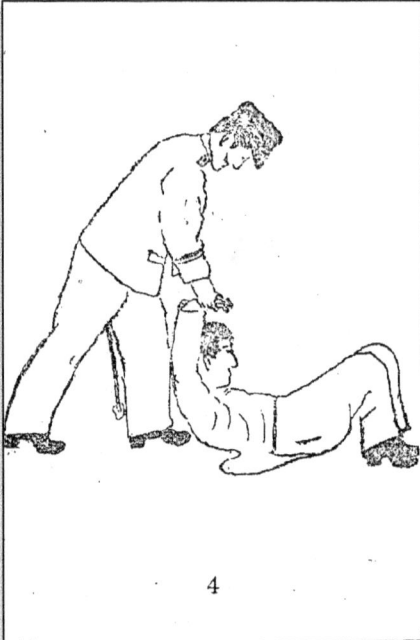

4

3

倒してから太刀をとる。

● 尚以下の制し方は第三技の變化技の何れ
を應用してもよい。

對手の右手を一旦左に逆にして倒したのを圖
の如く左膝外側部に當て更に右へ逆にとる。

（そうすると對手は自然に起き上らうとする）

150

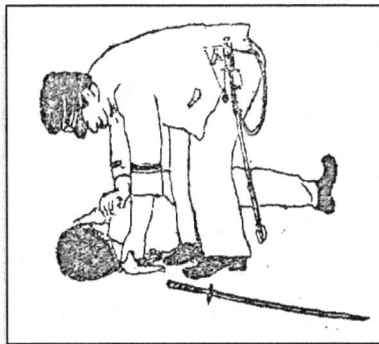

Illustration 3　　　　　　*Illustration 4*

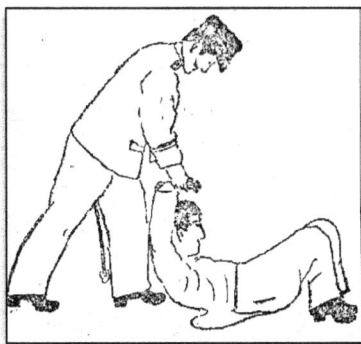

After you drop the suspect to the ground, take his sword.

- From this point onward, you can also use any of the Henka, or variations for technique #3.

As Illustration 4 shows, after initially twisting the suspect's right wrist to the left in a joint lock, you now twist it to the right as you place it against the outside of your left knee. (This will naturally cause the suspect to rise up off the ground.)

6

5

起き上る力を利用して圖の如く右手で對手の
右手を制しつゝ、前方に俯伏せに倒す樣にして

素早く對手の頭の方に左から廻つて對手の頸
を自分の左手で制しつゝ、圖の如く對手の頭部
を股に挾み右手を背に廻して充分制する。
（此の時右手を左手に取りかへれば反對に右
から廻つてもよい）

Illustration 5   *Illustration 6*

While maintaining control of the suspect's right arm with your right hand, use the motion of the suspect rising to flatten him face down on the ground in front of you.

Then, as Illustration 6 shows, rapidly move clockwise around so you are in front of the suspect's head. Control his neck with your left hand and keep his head positioned between your thighs. Twist the suspect's right arm behind his back sufficiently to maintain control.

(If you have taken the suspect's left arm instead of his right, then you would rotate counterclockwise around to the head.)

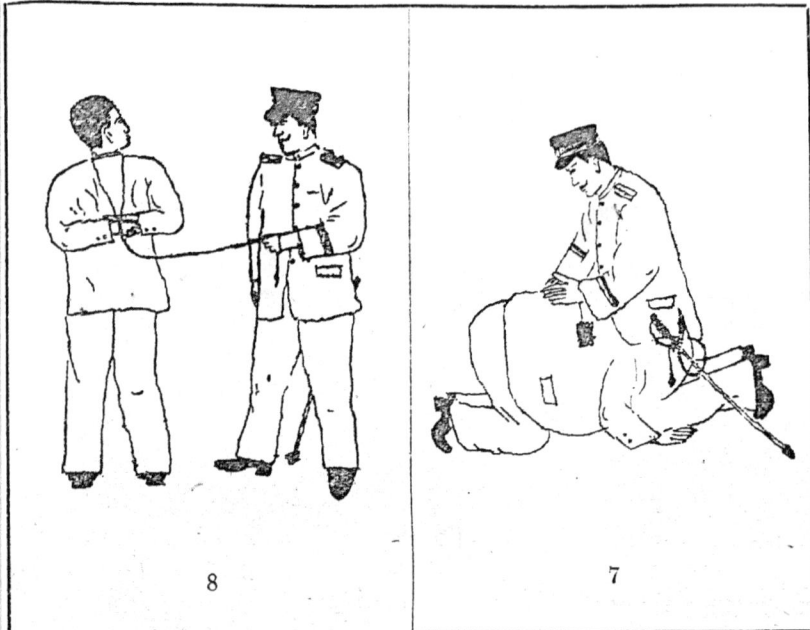

8

7

起たして連行する。

そして右手に捕繩をかけて左肩にかけ充分引
き上げて廻り左手をとつて背に廻し右手に重
ねて廻り頸にかけて充分制繩する。
（左肩に捕繩をかける時肩に深くかけること）

Illustration 7

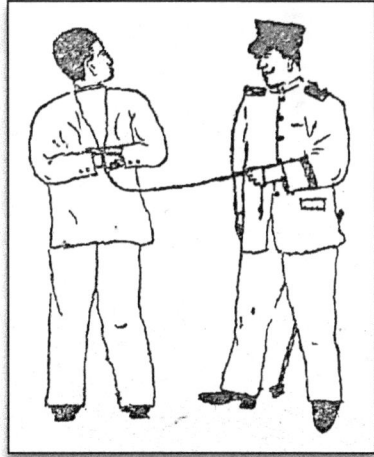

Illustration 8

Finally tie off the suspect's right hand and loop the rope over his left shoulder and pull his arm up his back sufficiently. Loop the rope around and, after placing his left hand on top of his right, tie him securely. Be sure the rope is applying appropriate pressure on the throat.

Bring the suspect to his feet and lead him away.

Supplemental Material
Hojo Jutsu : Using the Police Rope

（附録）

捕縄術の要領

捕縄術の要領

神道夢想流杖術師範
大日本武德會杖術教士
警察廰杖術教士

清水隆次氏講述

一、總說

捕縄にも長さにより色々に種別がある。普通皆様が使つて居らるゝのが三尋半であり、一番手輕く使ひ易いものである。長いものとして七尋半、九尋、十一尋と言ふ風に寸法が分かれて居る。

捕縄は少し太目のそして手頃のものを良とし、常に蛇口其の他の箇所が切れ易くなつては居ないかと言ふ事を點檢して、完全なものを持つて居ると同時に時々椿油を手に附けて扱ごくと軟かく具直ぐになり捌きよくなる。始終擦つて可愛がつてやるといざと言ふ時直ぐに役立つて呉れるものである。捕縄の使ひ方は恰も蛇が巻きつくと同じに一度巻きついたなら忽ち胴から首と見る間に巻きついて、動けなくしてしまふ樣に手に巻きつけたならば直ぐに頸足と言ふ風に次ぎ〳〵に巻きつけて自由を制縛してしまふ事が必要である。そして對手の力を次ぎ〳〵に殺いで行つて、丁度

二九

Supplemental Material: Hojo Jutsu, Using the Police Rope

Shindo Muso Ryu Jojutsu Shihan
Shinden Muso School Jo Senior Instructor
Dainihon Butokukai Jojutsu Kyoshi
All Japan Butokukai Jo Instructor
Keishicho Jojutsu Kyoshi
Police Department Jo Instructor
Transcript of a Lecture by Kiyomizu Takaji

1. General Outline

The length of the Hojo, police rope, can vary widely. The rope typically used is 3.5 fathoms, 6.3 meters, long, because that is the easiest to handle.[17] Longer ropes are divided into three categories: 7.5 fathoms, 9 fathoms and 11 fathoms.

The Hojo rope should be a little on the thick side and move easily across the hands. Before using your rope, always inspect it to ensure that there are no tears, particularly near the Snake's Mouth loop[18] at the end. Carrying a well-conditioned rope is essential, however you should also occasionally rub the rope with camphor oil. This will keep it soft, pliable and easy to work with. If you handle your rope with loving care then it will perform well for you when you are suddenly thrust into a situation.

---

[17] The author uses the word Hiro 尋. This is an old unit of measurement. 1 Hiro, or fathom, is equivalent to 180 centimeters or about 5.9 feet.

[18]

The *Jaguchi* 蛇口 snake's mouth is a loop on the end of the rope. It can either be pre-made (1) tied on the fly (2) or with a metal ring attached (3.)	1	2	3
	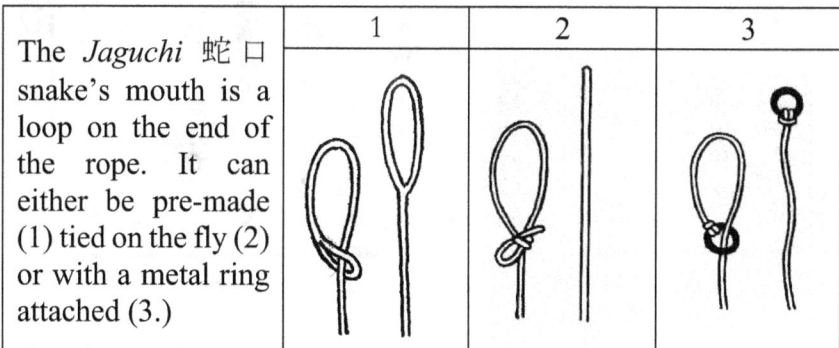		

赤子の手を捻む上る様に自由にしてしまふと言ふ所までに至らねばならぬ。柔道や剣道を應用するのも其處である。

昔の捕方が對手に對するとき先づ其の對手が強いか弱いかと言ふ事を見極めて、若し強い對手と見たならば之を根氣よく尾行して行つて其の隙と油斷とを見すまして やつたのである。例へば宿屋に泊つた時などに女中を買收して出來る丈澤山酒を呑まして貰つて酔ひ倒れて寝た所を見計つて刀をそつと取り上げてしまへ、そして捕縄を掛ける。立ち向つて來た時はすばやく足を拂ふと酔つて居るからすぐ倒れる、倒れた所を上から縄をかけてしまへふと云ふ方法をとつたものであつた。又昔は目潰し等も盛んに使用した。灰や砂や土、何でもよい一粒目に這入れば如何な剛のものでも目が見えなくなつてしまふ。

昔から極意と言ふ事を能く言つて居るのは一寸した所に注意を拂ふとか工夫をするとか、常人の思ひ及ばぬ點に妙用を發揮する所にあるのである。

或る人が私に「夜寝て居る時に強盗が這入つて來てホッと目を覺して見ると自分の胸へ七首を突き付けて居ると言ふ様な場合を想像して、その時果して、どうしたら

〇三

The Hojo rope is used in the same way a snake takes hold of its prey. When it wraps a creature up, a snake will, in one move, cover it in coils from waist to neck, rendering it immobile. Similarly, it is essential that when using the police rope, after tying the suspect's hands you immediately wrap the suspect up from neck to feet in a rapid series of motions, thereby completely removing the suspect's freedom of movement. By doing so you kill off any outlet for the criminal to make use of his power.

Just like you hold a baby's arms up to keep them still, it is essential that you completely remove a criminal's freedom of movement. Elements of Judo and Kendo will also be used in this course.

Long ago there was job called Torikata, or a person who captured criminals. If you were doing this job, you would first evaluate your opponent to determine his relative strength or weakness. If the subject seemed like a strong man, you would remain patient and trail the subject closely, waiting for an opportunity to catch him unaware.

For example, if the suspect were staying at an inn, you could bribe the hostess of the inn to give the target a large amount of Sake. When he eventually collapses from drunkenness, you could slip into the room he is staying, and take away his sword. Then you can tie him up.

If he should rise and charge you, respond by sweeping his feet out from under him. Since the man will be drunk, he will be easy to topple. After knocking him down you can mount him and tie him up. Of course, long ago they used Metsubushi, blinding powders, as the most effective way to stop a sudden attack. Blinding powders can be made from ash, sand, soil or other such ingredients. No matter how strong the man, if he gets a single grain in his eye, he will be rendered unable to see.

Long ago the ultimate display of skill was being aware of a problem only 1 Sun, or 3 centimeters, away from you and developing a solution to the problem then and there. You have to be able to solve the problem that is virtually right on top of you with a clever solution that would never occur to an average person.

よいだらうかと言ふことを此の間から大分考へて見たが、どうしてもかうすると言ふ考へが浮ばないが、如何したらよいだらうか」と言つて質問された事がある。私は『其の時は唾を對手の顔に吐きかける、そうすると賊はハッとして目を瞑る、その瞬間素早く小手を打つて七首を叩き落し、飛び起きて立ち向ふ。かうして間髪の間に危機を脱して攻勢に出ると言ふのも一つの方法である」と言つたら成る程と感心して居た事がある。或は亦拳銃を擬して迫つて來た場合を考へても初めは兩手を上げて害心なき風を裝ひ、接近して來た時に唾を顔に吐きかける、對手がハッとした瞬間その腕關節を高く差し上る様にとると拳銃は空を撃つ同時に當身を喰はして投げつけて取押へると云ふ風に其の瞬間を利用すると言ふ事が大切である。之等は一例であるが、極意とか、奥儀とか言ふのも要するにかうした小さい所から生れて來ると思ふ。

二、捕縄術の種類

捕縄術は其の基本及び用途によつて引致縄、早縄、護送縄に分かれ、その内が又數種に分類される。

The other day, an acquaintance of mine said, "I was thinking of a situation where a thief crept into my house while I was asleep. Waking with a start, I realize he had a knife pressed against my chest. I wondered what I could do in such a situation. What action could I take? No matter how much I thought about it I couldn't come up with a solution. Do you have any idea what I could do in such a situation?"

I thought about his problem for a little and then answered him, "Spit in the thief's face. This swill startle him and momentarly cloud his vision. Use that moment to rapidy strike his wrist, knocking his knife from his hand. Then leap up and face him. This is one method of going on the offensive that will allow you to escape a life or death situation."

My aquaintance, nodded in understanding and was very interested in this solution.

Another situation you can consider is if a man is advancing on you with what appears to be a pistol. You should initally respond by raising both hands as if you have no intention of resisting. When he comes in range spit in his face. The moment he reacts in surprise, shove his elbow up in the air. As his pistol fires up in the air, you make him eat your fist before throwing him down and securing him. In other words, it is important to make use of that single moment as described above.

These are just a couple of examples however the essesnse or inner mystries of responding to sudden attack. A small thing can be the solution in an extreme situation.

2. Types of Hojo Jutsu

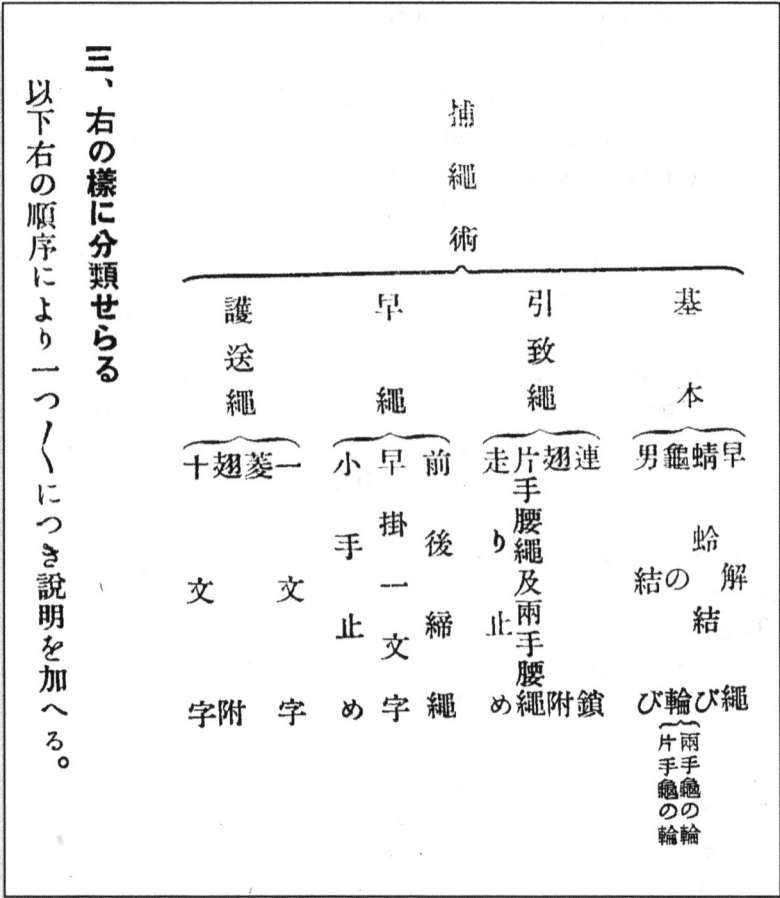

捕縄術

基本
　早解縄
　蜻蛉結び縄
　男龜結び輪
　　両手龜の輪
　　片手龜の輪

引致縄
　連り止め
　翅り止め
　片手腰縄及両手腰縄附鎖
　走り

早縄
　早掛一文字
　小手止め

護送縄
　一文字
　菱文字
　翅文字
　十文字附

三、右の様に分類せらる

以下右の順序により一つ〳〵につき説明を加へる。

164

2. Types of Hojo Jutsu

There are fundamentals to securing suspects with rope and different categories depending on what your objective is. For example Arresting Tie, Quick Tie and Prisoner Transport Tie. These and other subdivisions are shown in the chart below.

Hojo Jutsu Rope Binding Techniques			
Part 4	Part 3	Part 2	Part 1
Prisoner Transport Tie	Fast Rope	Arresting Rope	Basic
One Line	Front & Back Tie	Continuous Chain	Quick Release Rope
Water Caltrop	One Line Fast Tie	Folded Wings	Dragonfly Tie
Folded Wings	Wrist Lock	One-handed Waist Tie & Two-handed Waist Tie	Two-Handed Turtle Loop & One-Handed Turtle Loop
Cross Shaped		Stop Running	Men's Tie

3. Breakdown and Explanation of the Above Chart
The following pages will detail each of these categories and sub-categories.

Part 1 : Fundamentals
1. Quick Release Rope

Part 1 : Fundamentals
1. Quick Release Rope

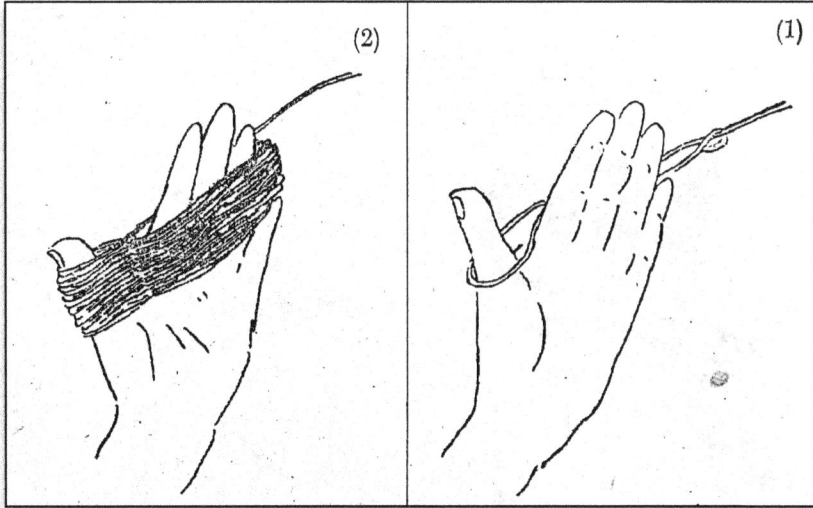

Quick Release Rope is how you prepare your Hojo, police rope, before you tie a person. This is a method for wrapping the rope around your fingers so that it can be used immediately. If you prepare the rope like this, it will unravel smoothly.

1. Hook the Jaguchi, Snake's mouth, around the thumb of your left hand. This is shown in the first illustration.
2. Starting from the back of the hand, wrap the rope towards the inside of your palm. Pass it outside and around your thumb before bringing it over the back of your hand again. Continue in this fashion until about 2 Shaku, 60 centimeters remain.

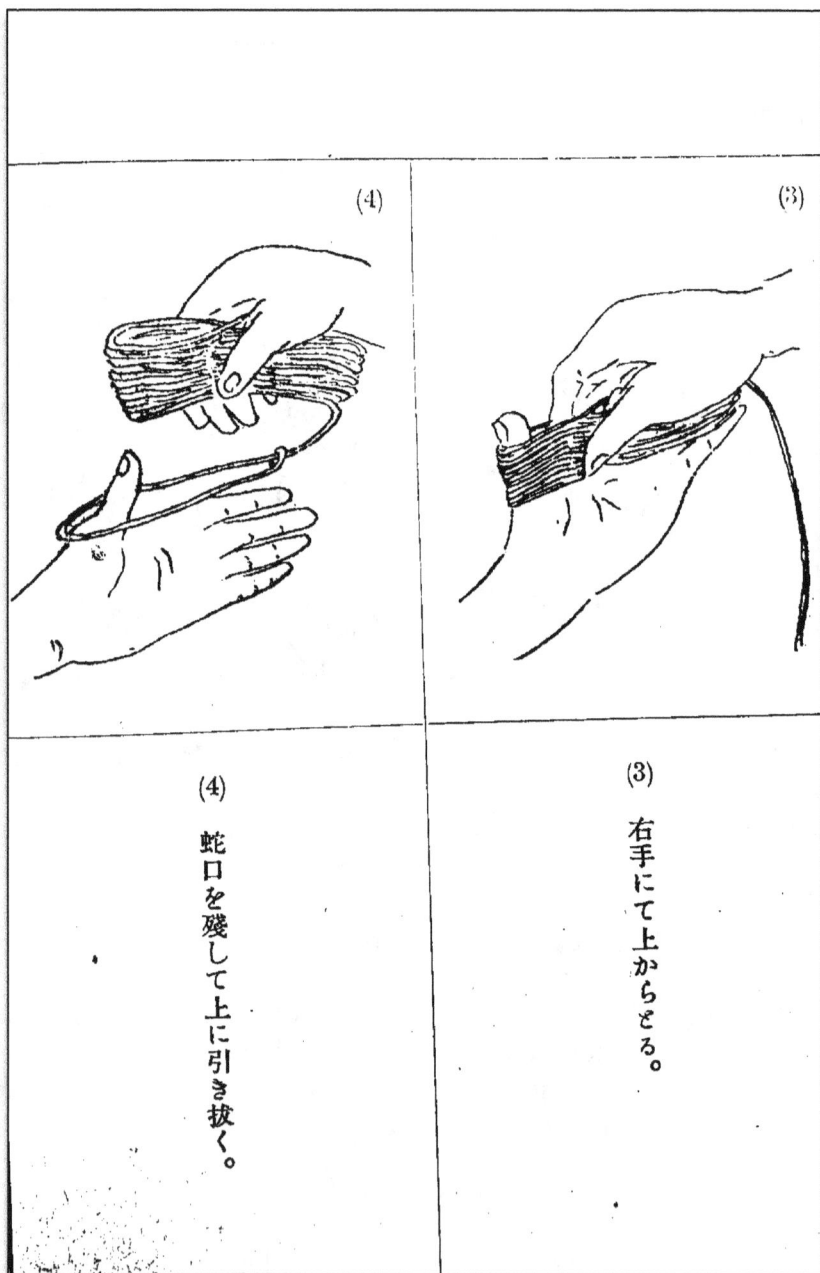

(4)

(3)

(4)
蛇口を殘して上に引き抜く。

(3)
右手にて上からとる。

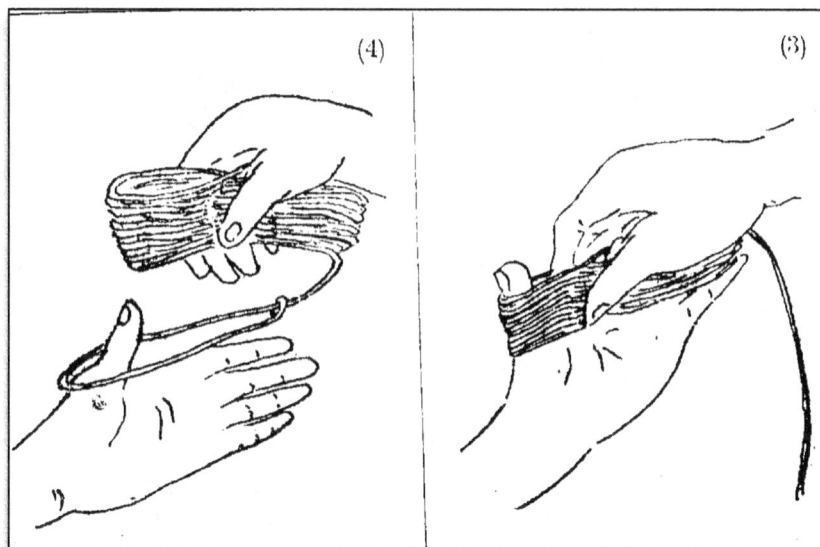

3. Grab it with your right hand from above.
4. Remove the rope, leaving the Snake's Mouth hooked on your thumb.

(6)

(5)

(6)
殘した端で二つに折つたのを巻き終り端をはせ込んで止めると出來上る
蛇口の所は直ぐ使用に便なる様殘しておく。
蛇口の方からスルゝと抜けて來て直ちに捕縄として捕縛に使用出來る

(5)
上に引き抜いて左手を添へて二つに折る。
蛇口の所を必ず下向けに折り曲げること。

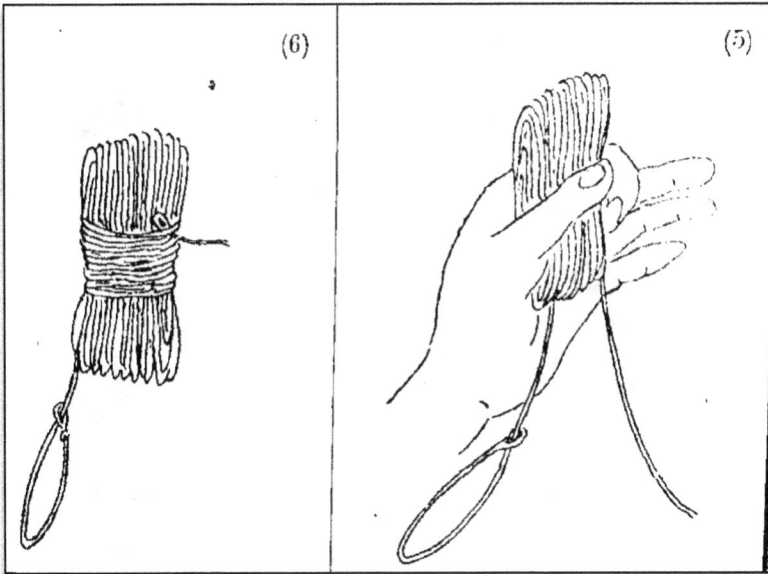

5. After lifting the rope up, fold the coil in half and take it in your left hand. Ensure that the Snake's Mouth loop is hanging downward after you fold the rope.
6. Wrap the remaining rope around the doubled coil of rope, and wedge the end into the wrapping. Leave the Snake's Mouth as it is so that you can easily make use of the rope. The rope will play out smoothly when you pull on the Snake's Head enabling you to immediately use the cord to tie the suspect.

2.蜻蛉結び

(2)

(1)

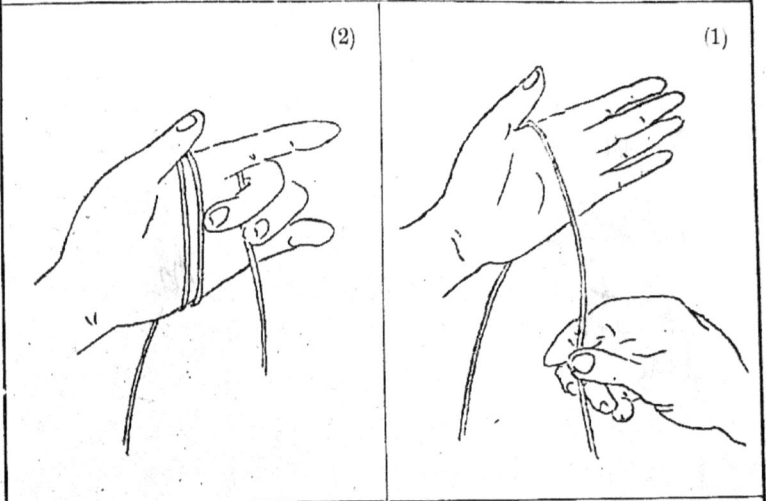

蜻蛉結びは両手を縛する時や連鎖に使用するに便なる様な結び方である。

(1) 左手に圖の様に捕繩をかけ內から外へ。

(2) 二つ卷き三つ目を示指と中指との間から內へ拔き。

— 8 —

172

2. Dragonfly Knot

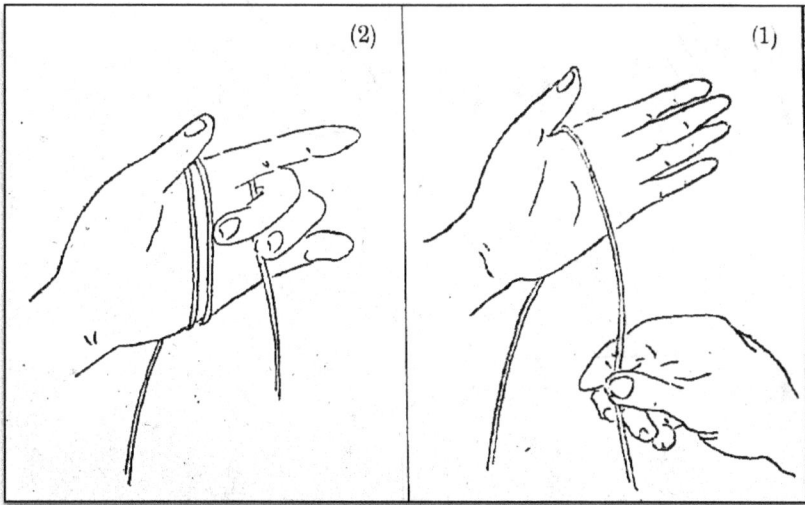

Tonbo Musubi, Dragonfly Knot, is used to tie both hands together. It is also a useful knot for tying together multiple people in a row.

1. Start as shown in the first illustration. Hold the rope in your left hand and wrap it from the inside to the outside.
2. Wrap the rope twice and on the third turn wrap it between your index finger and middle finger.

(4) (3)

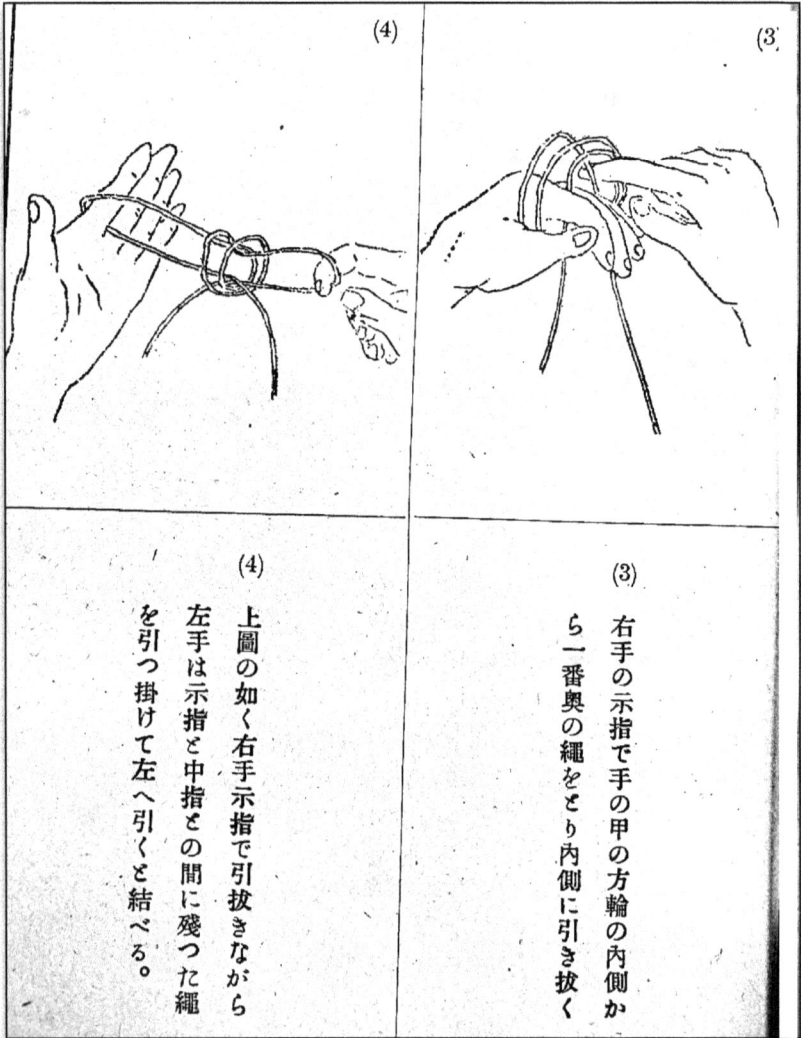

(4)

上圖の如く右手示指で引抜きながら
左手は示指と中指との間に殘つた繩
を引つ掛けて左へ引くと結べる。

(3)

右手の示指で手の甲の方輪の内側か
ら一番奥の繩をとり内側に引き抜く

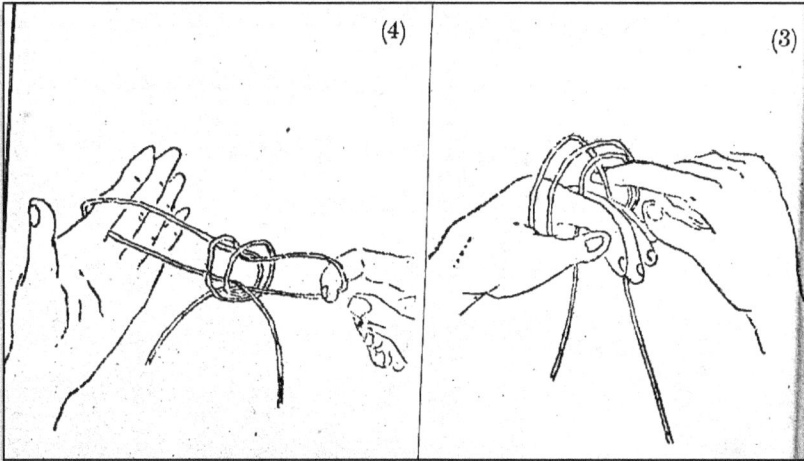

3. Use the index finger of your right hand to reach through the rope coiled around the back of your left hand and pull the backmost strand forward.

4. As the illustration shows, pull with your right index finger while you pull in the opposite direction with your left hand. Your left hand is holding only the strand between your middle and index fingers. This will tie the knot.

(5)

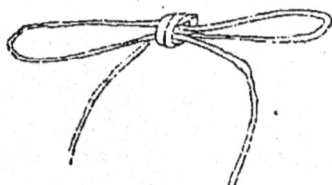

(5)

出來上り

両方の輪に両手或は二人の片手づゝ
を入れて両端を引けば締まる。

充分緊めてから最後に男結びをして
止めることを忘れぬこと。

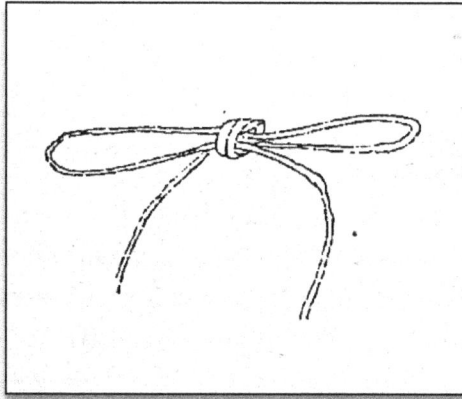

5.   The final knot should look like this.

You can slip both hands of one suspect or, alternately, one hand each of two suspects through the loops. By pulling tight on the ends, the rope will tighten.

Be sure to tighten the loops securely and don't forget to finish by adding a Men's Knot[19] to the end.

---

[19]Otoko Mususbi (Men's Knot,) Other names for this knot include Kakine Musubi (Fence Knot,) Moro Musubi (Double Knot,) Ibo Musubi (Wart Knot,) An Mususbi (Hermitage Knot,) Shiori (Garden Gate Knot) and Hae-gashira (Fly's Head Knot.)

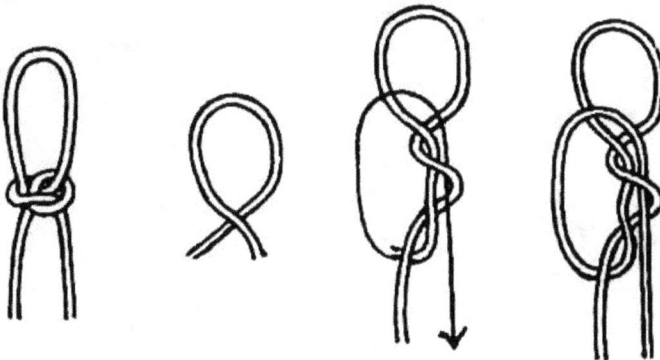

3. Turtle Loop
Both Hands

3. 龜の輪

イ、兩手

(1)

(1) 上圖の如く左手に繩を掛け右手は逆に繩をとる。

龜の輪は主として片手づゝと言ふ様に一つのものを縛るに用ひ一番多く使はれるものである。

兩手龜の輪は兩手を使つて作るのである

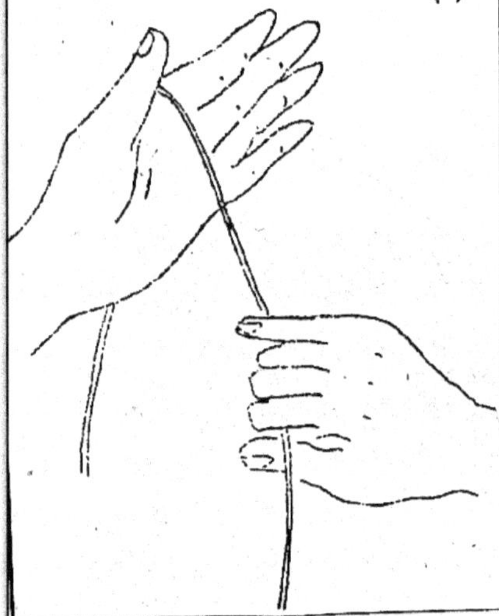

3. Turtle Loop
Both Hands

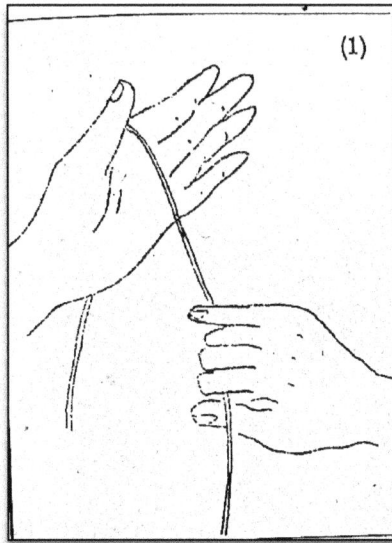

1. As the illustration shows, hold the rope in your left hand and, with your right hand in a reverse grip, take hold of the other end.[20]

A Kame no Wa, Turtle Loop, is used to tie off each hand. This tie is typically used to tie off one thing. Both hands are used when tying a two-handed Turtle Loop.

---

[20] The author uses the words Gyaku and Jun, to refer to a reverse grip and a regular grip.

Gyaku 逆 Reverse   Jun 順 Regular

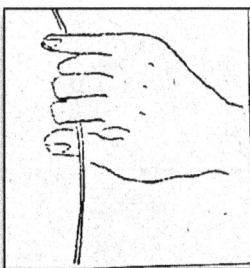

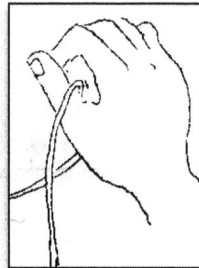

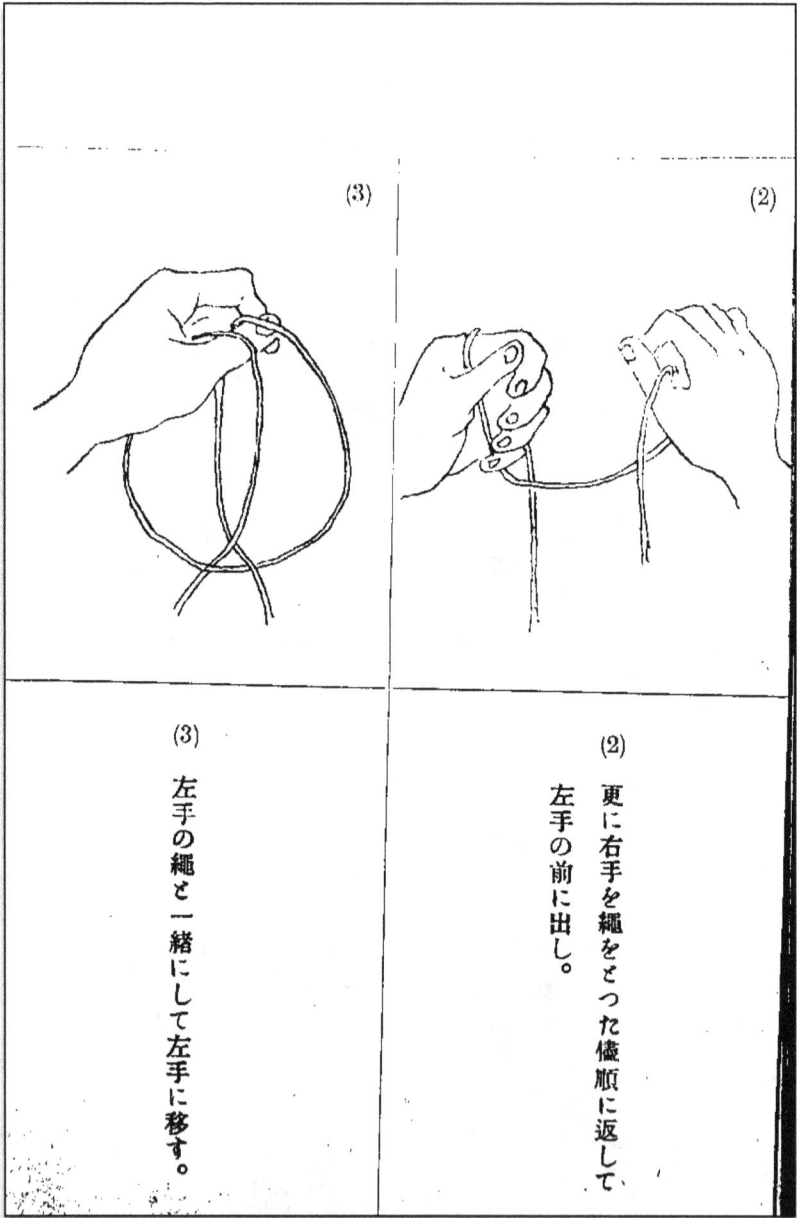

(3)

(2)

(3)

左手の縄と一緒にして左手に移す。

(2)

更に右手を縄をとった儀順に返して左手の前に出し。

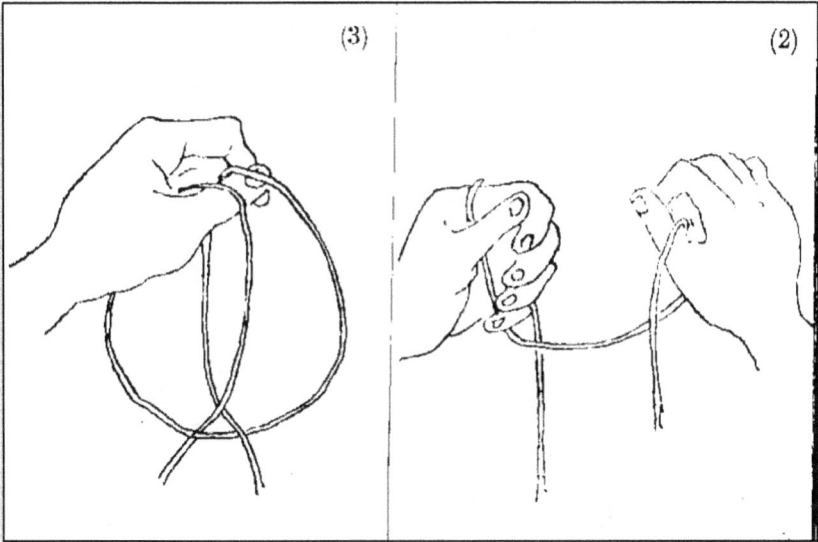

2. After taking the rope in your right hand, rotate your right hand up and in front of your left hand.
3. Move the piece of rope from your right hand to your left.

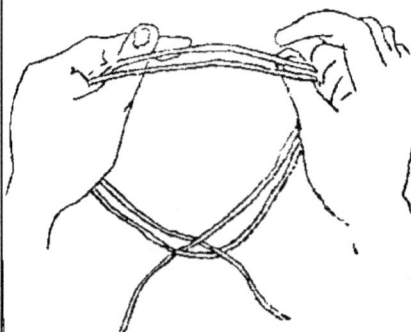

(4)

そして左手拇子で開くと龜の輪が出
來上る。

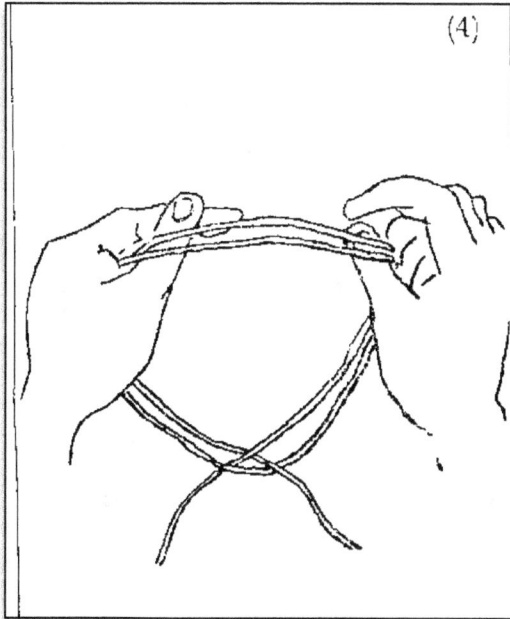

4. Use your left thumb to open up the loop and the Turtle Loop is finished.[21]

---

[21] The author may have meant "use *both* thumbs."

Turtle Loop
One-Handed

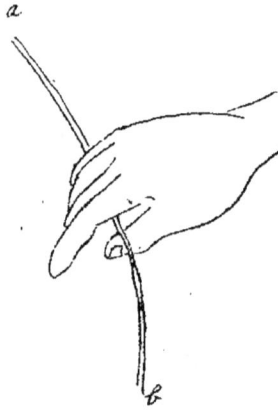

ロ、片手

(1)

a
b

(1)
片手龜の輪は片手で作るのであり一
方の手では對手を押へつけておると
云ふ様な場合、兩手で作る事が出來
ない時に應用され最も便利な方法で
ある。
縄の何處でもよい兎に角縄の端さへ
圖の如く右手で逆に取ればよい。
（左手の時も同様である）

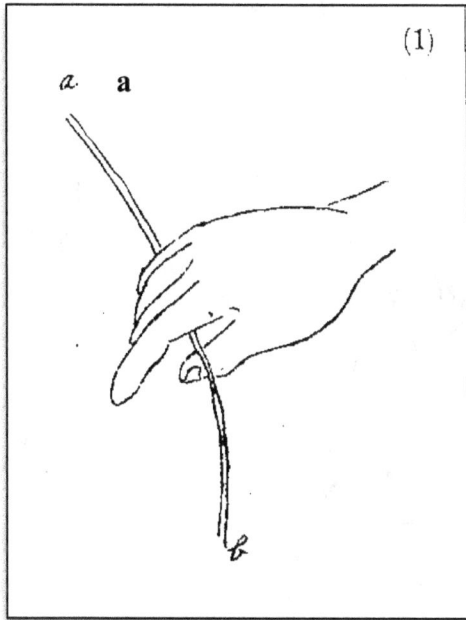

Turtle Loop
One-Handed

1. Kata-te Kame no Wa, One-Handed Turtle Loop is made with one hand. This is because this knot is typically employed when you are using one hand to hold down the suspect. Thus, when you have one hand occupied this is the best way to make a knot one-handed.

   It doesn't matter what part of the rope you use, even the end of the rope. Take hold of it with your right hand in a reverse grip as shown in the illustration.

   (This is done the same way if you are using your left hand.)

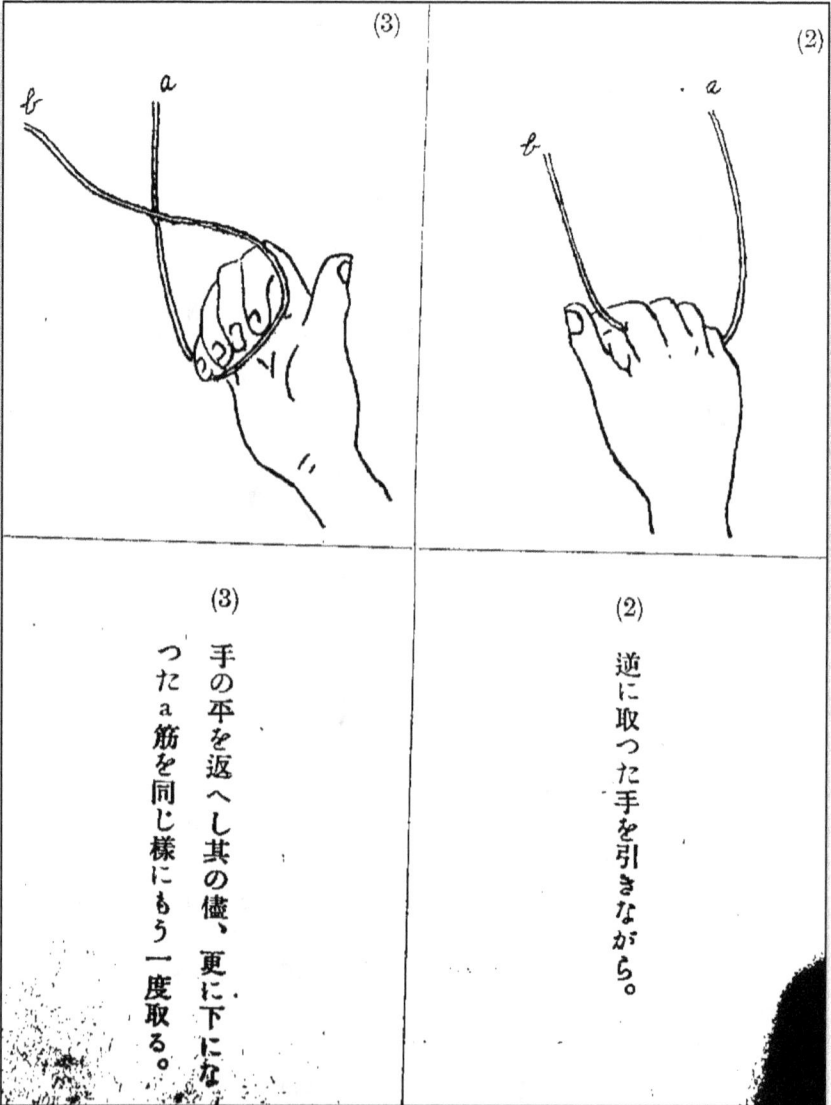

(3)

(2)

(3)

手の平を返へし其の儘、更に下にな
つた a 筋を同じ様にもう一度取る。

(2)

逆に取つた手を引きながら。

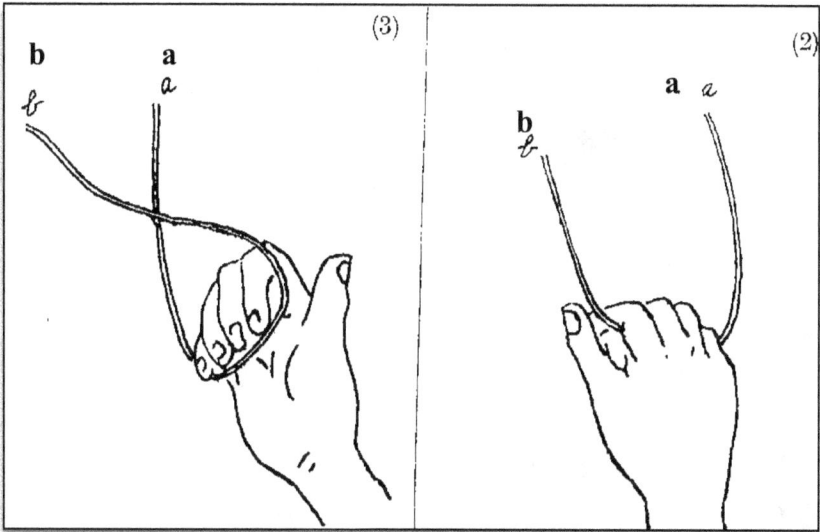

2. Pull with the hand you grabbed the rope in a reverse grip…
3. …and rotate your hand over horizontally. Next take hold of strand (a) that is now below (b) in the same manner.

4.
男
結
び

(1)

(4)

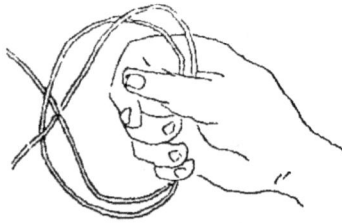

(4)
出
来
上
り

直
ぐ
に
も
一
方
の
手
で
押
へ
付
け
て
居
る

對
手
の
手
首
な
り
、
足
な
り
へ
引
つ
掛
け

る
こ
と
が
出
来
る
。

(1)

男
結
び
は
蜻
蛉
結
び
や
、
龜
の
輪
を
利
用
し
て

縛
つ
た
後
結
び
止
め
を
し
て
緩
ま
な
い
様
に
す

る
結
び
方
で
あ
る
。

何
處
で
も
よ
い
締
め
た
両
端
を
圖
の
如
く

一
方
を
輪
に
す
る
。

188

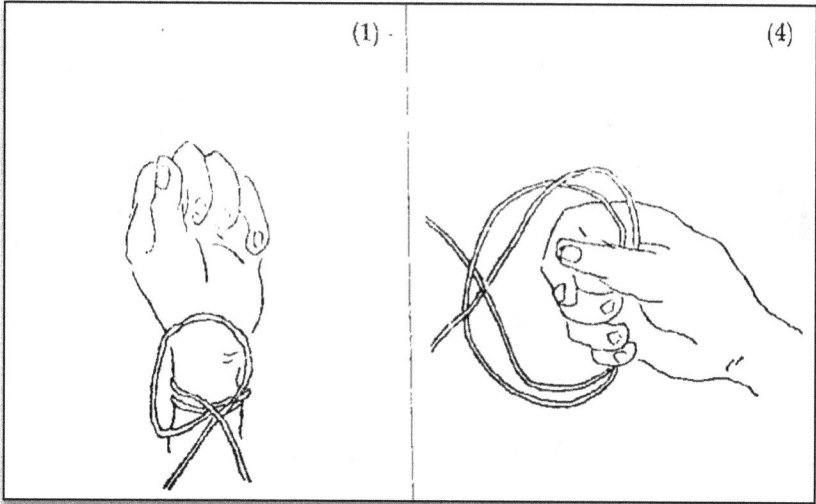

4. The finished knot should look like this.

This can be tied quickly with one hand and applied to the suspect's wrist or ankle while your other hand is holding the suspect down.

4. Men's Knot

Otoko Musubi, Men's Knot, is used after tying either a Dragonfly Tie or Turtle Ring. It serves to prevent those ties from coming loose.
  1. The knot can be made anywhere on the tie. Take both ends of the rope you have pulled tight and make a loop with one.

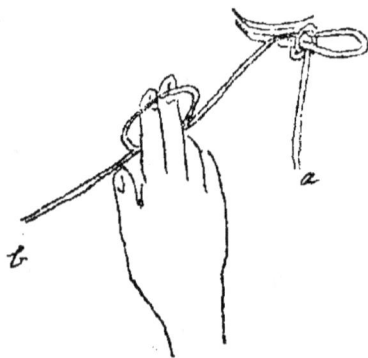

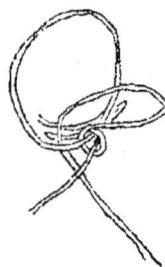

(3)

上圖の如く結んだ儘ではb筋を引け
ばほどけるからb筋の方を右手示指
と中指二本の指で圖の如く輪を作り

(2)

輪にしない一方を輪にした方に締め
て差し込み、輪にした方の一方を引
張るさ(3)の如く結べる。

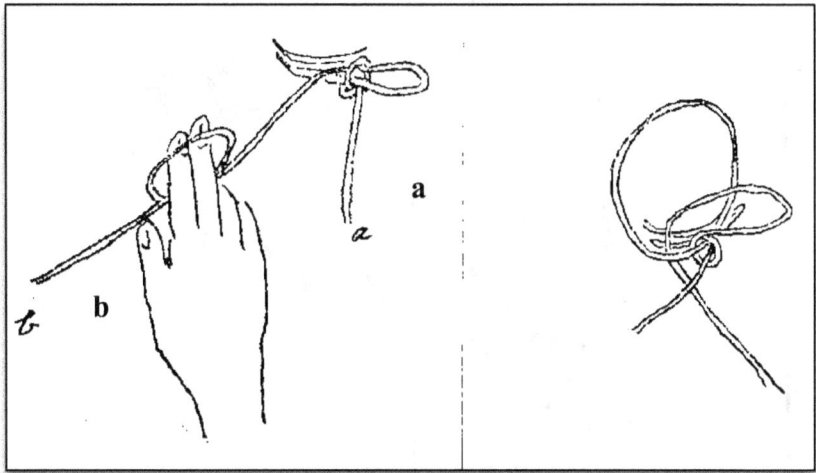

2. Push a section of the rope you did not make a loop out of through the loop. Pull the end of the rope you made a loop with and you will end up with a tie that looks like what is shown in Illustration 3.

3. If you leave the tie as shown in Illustration 3, then by pulling on (b) the whole thing will come undone. So make a loop on that part of the rope with your index and middle fingers.

(5)

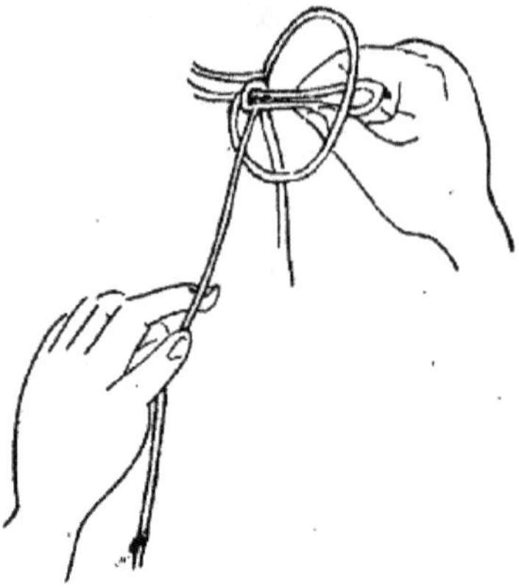

(4)

(4)

結び目に差入れてb筋を引けば締
つてa、b筋何れを引いてもほど
けない

(5)

出来上り
兩方の繩をいくら引張つてもほど
けない

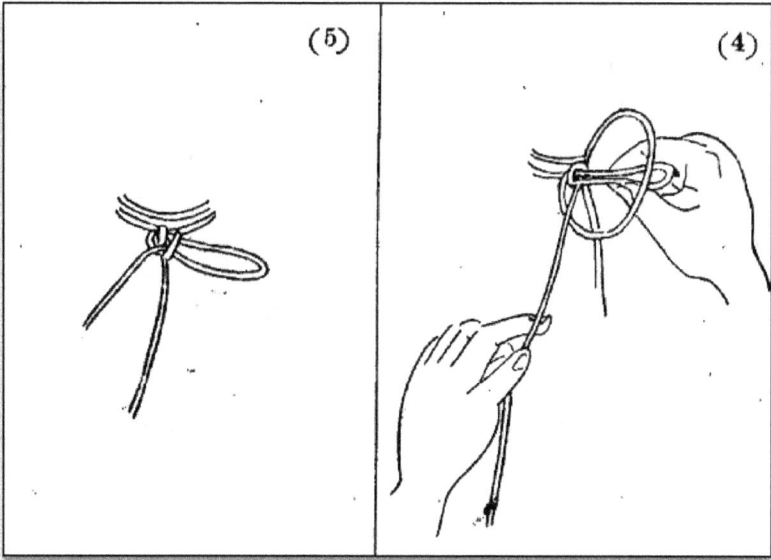

4. Slip the loop you made with your two fingers into the tie you made. By pulling (b) tight, even if you pull on strands (a) or (b) the knot will not release.
5. The finished tie should look like this.
   No matter how much you pull on either end, the tie will not come undone.[22]

22

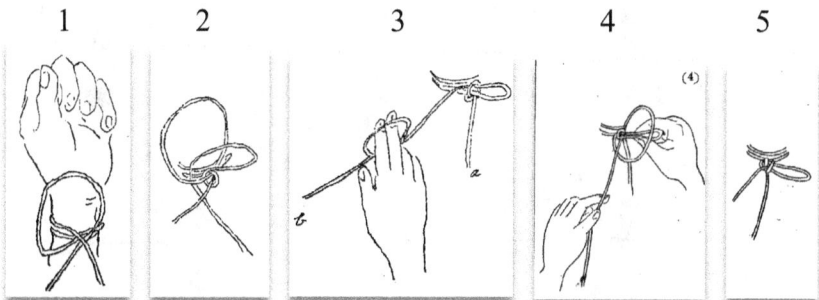

JAPANESE POLICE MANUAL

Part Two : Arrresting Rope

二、引致縄

1. 連　鎖

イ、蜻蛉結びを利用する連鎖

数人の者を同時に制縛する連鎖の方法に蜻蛉結びを利用するものと、龜の輪を利用する場合と二種類ある

(1) 蜻蛉結びの兩方の輪に片手づゝを入れて締め、一連毎に男結びにて止め次の蜻蛉結びを作る

(2) 締めた最後に男結びにて止めて次の蜻蛉結びをすることを忘れないこと。若し男結びを忘れると自然に緩む恐がある

四五

194

Part Two : Arrresting Rope

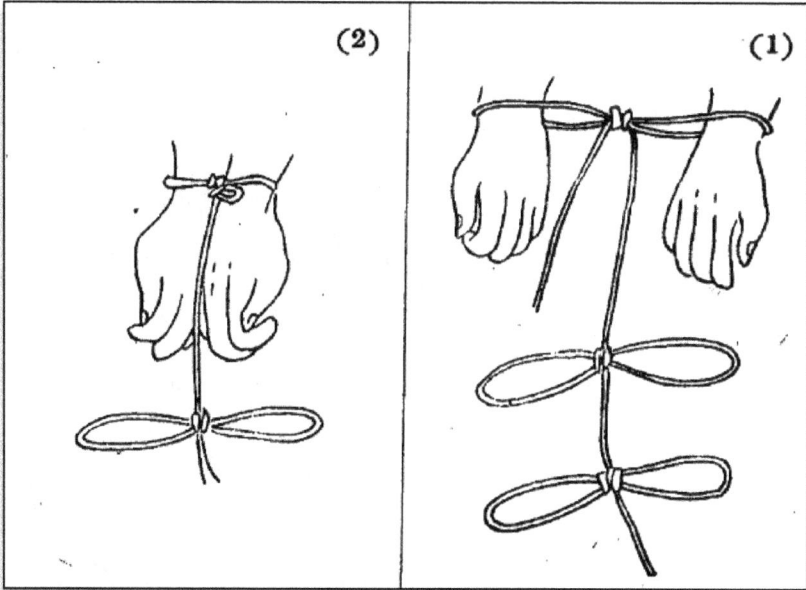

1. Chain Tie
Using Dragonfly Tie to Tie Together Multiple Suspects

When you need to restrain multiple people at the same time with rope, there are two types of ties you can use, Dragonfly Tie or Turtle Tie.

1. When using Tonbo Musubi, Dragonfly Tie, place one hand inside each loop and then tighten. After tying the first person, finish with a Men's knot before making the next Dragonfly Tie.

2. Be sure to not forget to tie a Men's Knot after you tighten down the Dragonfly Tie. If you forget the Men's Knot the rope will naturally loosen.

Using Turtle Loop To Secure Multiple Supects

ロ、龜の輪を利用する連鎖

(1)
龜の輪を作り之に片手づ、或は、兩手一緒でもよい差入れて締め、連續に幾つでも龜の輪を作り連鎖に利用する。

(2)
此の場合も一連毎に男結びに止めてから次の龜の輪を作ること、二つの手を一緒に差入れたときは其の眞中に更に繩を通して締めておくこと。

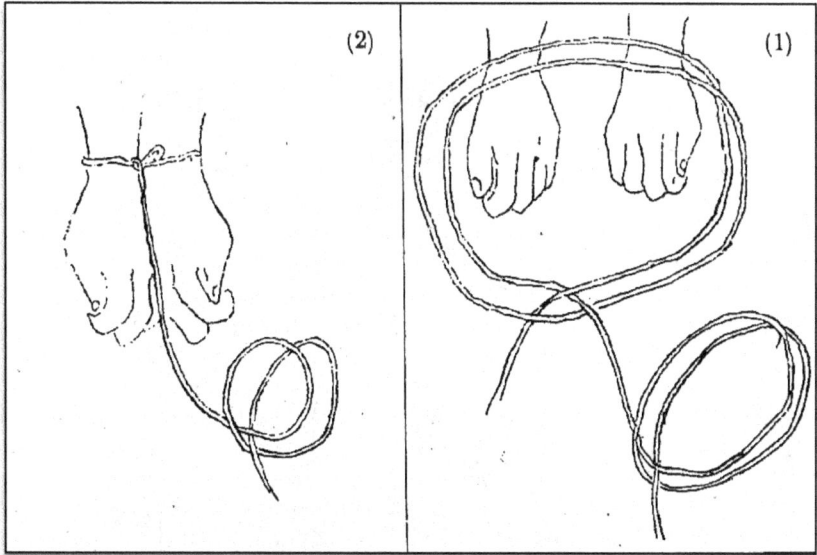

Using Turtle Loop To Secure Multiple Supects

1. You can make a Kame no Wa, Turtle Loop to secure one or both hands of a suspect. After pulling it tight you can continue making as many Turtle Loops as you need to secure suspects in a chain.

2. When doing this you should tie a Men's Knot after each person is secured, then make the next Turtle Loop. When securing both hands be sure to wrap the rope in between the hands to secure them tightly.

II. Folded Wings

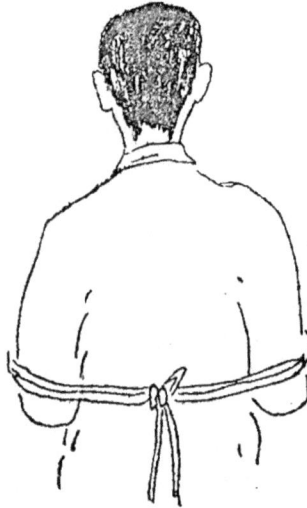

2.
翅
附

大きい龜の輪を作り、後からスッポリか
ぶせ込み、兩肘關節の稍々上部を胴體に
密着する樣緊縛する。
良く締めて男結びとする。
翅附は泥醉者等の暴行を制する時に利用
して便利である。

II. Folded Wings

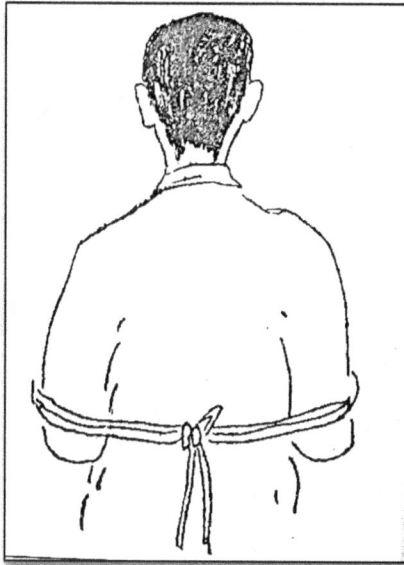

II. Folded Wings

Make a large Turtle Loop and, standing behind the suspect, slide it over his body. Tighten the rope slightly above the elbows ensuring they are pressed firmly against the body.

After tightening the rope, finish with a Men's Knot. This tie is convenient for securing violent people, like drunks.

III. One-handed Waist Tie

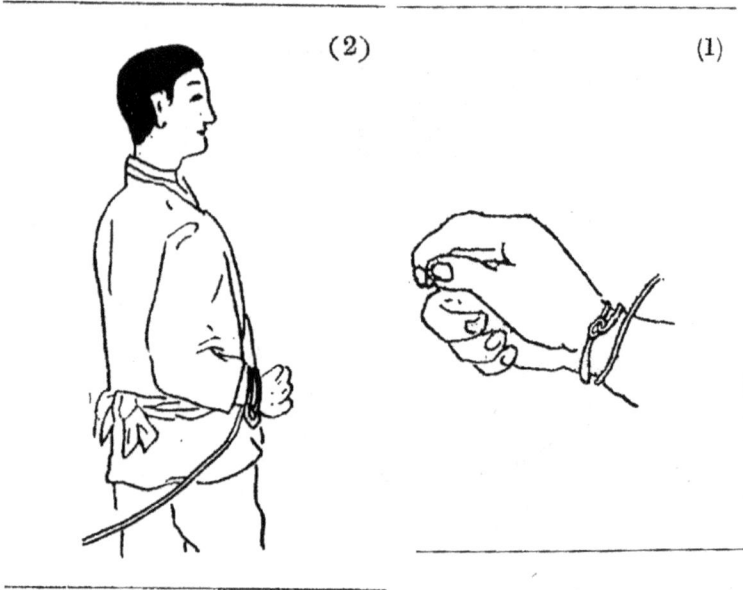

3. 片手腰繩
両手腰繩

(2) (1)

(1)

捕繩を蛇口に通し片手の手頸に入れ
二卷き卷いて。

(2) 更に帶に通して緊縛す

兩手腰繩

兩手腰繩は繩の殘り片方を後ろから
一方の手の方に廻し片手腰繩の要領
にて緊縛するのである

III. One-handed Waist Tie

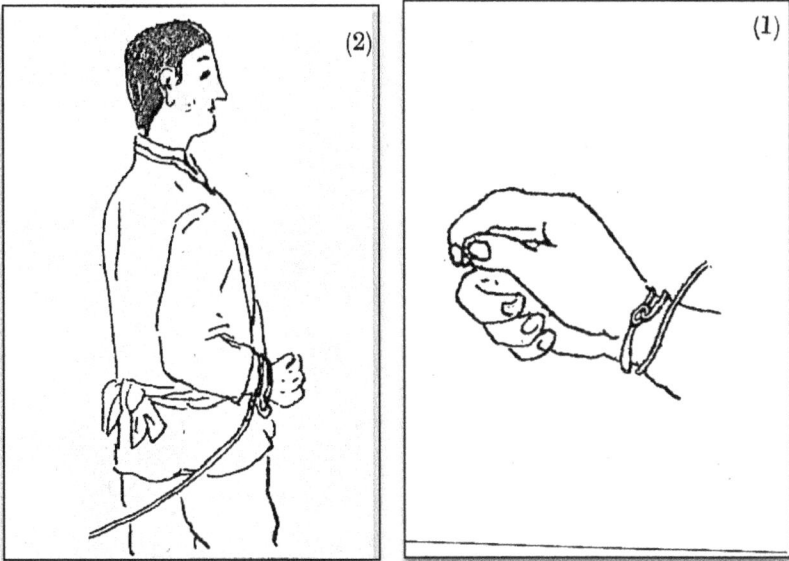

III. One-Handed & Two-Handed Waist Tie

One-Handed Waist Tie

1. Pass the rope through the Jaguchi, Snake's Head loop on the end of your rope. Wrap the loop around the suspect's wrist and wrap it twice.
2. Next, pass the rope through the suspect's belt.

Two-handed Waist Tie

To make a Two-Handed Waist Tie, take the rope remaining from One-Handed Waist Tie and wrap it around the suspects back. Then Tie of his other hand in One-Handed Waist Tie.

4. Stop From Running Away

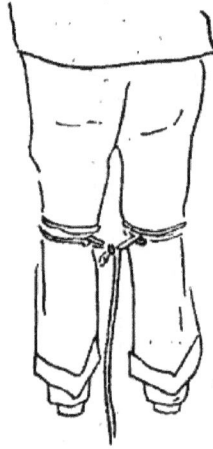

走り止めは逃走を防ぐ爲め兩膝關節の部分を歩行の出來る程度に少しく餘裕を置き兩足を縛するのである

着物の下から外見上わからない樣にして縛し連行するに便利である

片足づ〻龜の輪を應用して縛つて止め更に片足を同樣縛つて兩足を連結する

（强盗犯人等の被害附けに連行する場合等に應用）

4. 走り止め

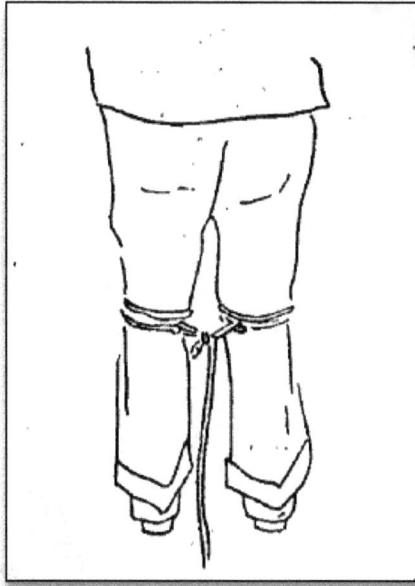

4. Stop From Running Away

Hashiri Tome, Stop From Running Away, is a tie used to prevent suspects from escaping. Both knees are tied with just enough slack to allow a suspect to walk.

If you tie the suspect under their Kimono,[23] then from the outside, people will not notice that the person you are escorting is restrained. Apply this by using a Turtle Ring tie on each leg. This will mean each leg is tied and that they are both tied together.

(This tie is good for when you are escorting armed robbers and other such criminals to the scene of the crime.)

---

[23] In this case the word Kimono could mean a Japanese style Kimono or just clothing in general.

Part 3 : Fast Tie

Part 3 : Fast Tie

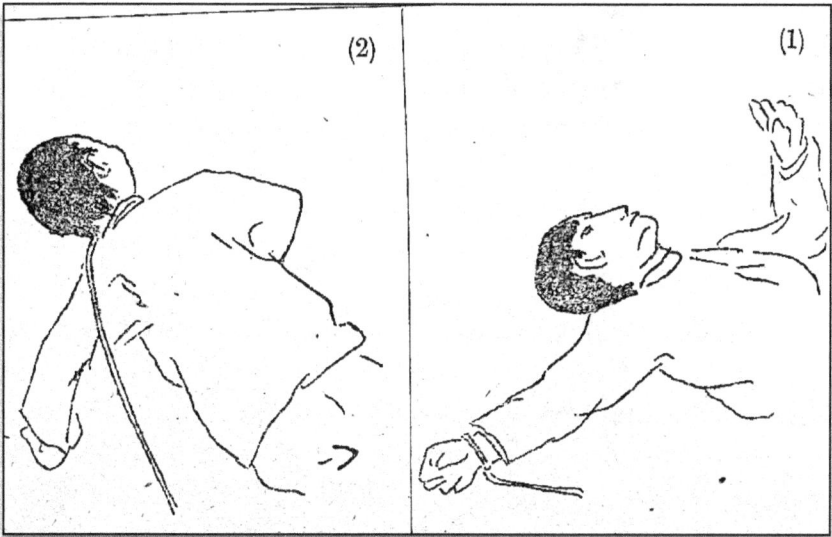

1. Front Back Secure Tie

1. For a suspect that has been thrown down on his back, first tie off his right hand.
2. After tying off his right hand rapidly pass the rope over his left shoulder and around his neck while turning him over onto his stomach.

2. Straight Line Fast Tie

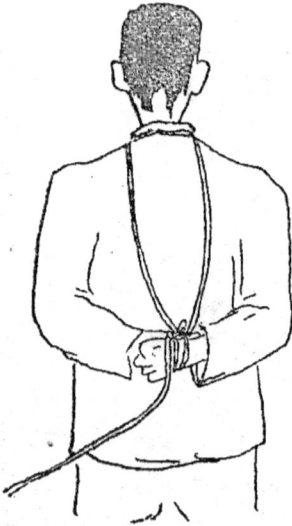

2. 早掛一文
字

(3)

左手を捻ぢ上げて肩から廻して來た
繩で縛つて止める。

右手は前で左手は後ろで縛る。

良く繩を引張つて締めつけないと綏
み易い。

(3)

兩手を後に縛し後ろから頸にかけ襷に通
して緊縛する。繩を掛ける時はあぐらを
かゝして置くこと、立膝は對手が自由に
體を變化させて抵抗或は逃走を企てしむ
る虞がある。

天狗倒し
背後から兩耳のあたりを兩平手にて下
から叩き上げる様、打ち對手がハッと
した瞬間兩足を後ろから兩手にて刈り
込んで前方に倒し兩手を逆にとつて捕
繩をかける、早掛一文字は之を應用す
る。

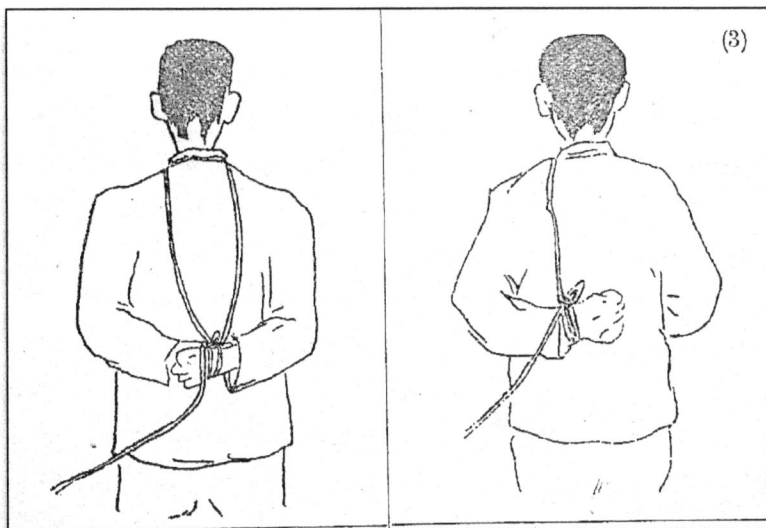

3. Twist his left hand up behind his back and tie it off with the rope you brought over his shoulder.
   You have tied his right hand in front of him and his left hand behind him. If you do not ensure there is sufficient tension on the rope this tie can come loose.

2. Straight Line Fast Tie

Haya Nawa Ichi Monji, Straight Line Fast Tie is a tie that first wraps both hands behind the back before running the rope around the neck and then securing to the belt. When tying this be sure to make the suspect sit Agura, or cross-legged. If you allow the suspect to sit Tate-hiza, or with the knees drawn up, he will have sufficient freedom of movement to attempt to resist or escape.

Tengu Taoshi : Felling the Mountain Goblin

Approach your opponent from behind. With the palms of both hands held open and flat strike his ears up from below. Your opponent will be shocked for a moment, use that moment to sweep both of his legs from behind by seizing his legs with your hands. This will cause him to fall forward. Use your hands to take a joint lock on him as you tie him up with your arresting rope. Straight Line Fast Tie can be applied in this situation.

3. 小手止め

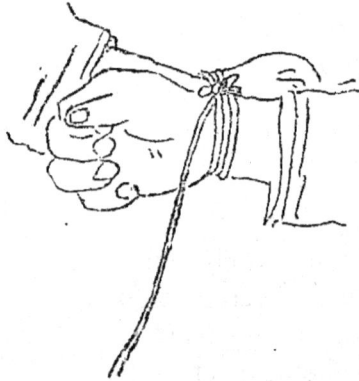

両手を後ろ手に縛することは早掛一文字と同様であるが捕縄を頸に掛けないで小手のみを止める先づ右手を蛇口或は鰌の輪を應用して縛り左手を上に重ね、右手と共に縛る、此の時兩手首の關節の所を合して縛らないと緩む又更に兩手を縛つた間に繩を差し入れて縛つて置けば尚充分である。

後ろ手でなく前で縛ることもある、要領は同様である。

（圖では右手が上になつて居るが右手を下にすれば尚効果的である）

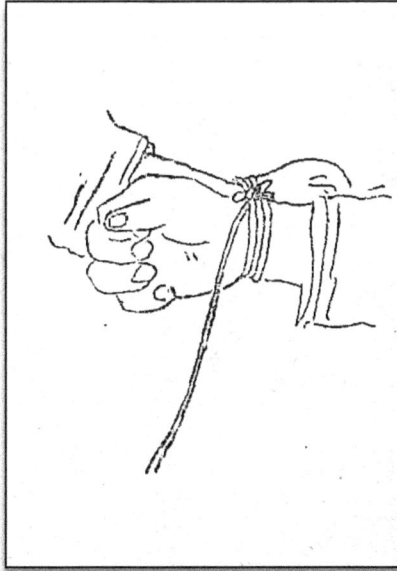

3. Wrist Fastener

Kote-dome, Wrist Fastener, is similar to Haya Nawa Ichi Monji, Straight Line Fast Tie, since you are tying both hands behind the back. However, in this tie the rope does not go around the neck, but only ties the wrists.

To tie Wrist Fastener, first use the Snake's Mouth or tie a Turtle Loop to tie the suspect's right wrist. Then place the suspect's left wrist on top of his right and tie the two hands together. When doing this if you do not overlay the wrists, the knot may become loose. However, you can solve this problem when tying the wrists by wrapping the rope several turns between the wrists.

The hands can also be tied in front in addition to behind the back. (The illustration shows the right hand on top, however this technique is most effective with the right hand behind the left.)

Part 4 : Prisoner Transport Tie
1. Straight Line

四、護送繩

1. 一文字

早掛一文字と同様であるが、早掛の方は捕繩する場合であり、早く掛ける事を必要とする為、両手を縛る場合も早きを尊ぶが護送繩の場合は一層入念に緊縛するだけである。

Part 4 : Prisoner Transport Tie
1. Straight Line

This technique is similar to Hayanawa Ichimonji, Straight Line Fast Tie, however this technique is not focused on speed as the latter is. When in a situation that requires speed, the focus is on tying both the suspect's hands in a short amount of time.   For Prisoner Transport Tie, you are primarily concerned with tying the prisoner securely.

2. Water Chestnut
3. Folded Wings

3.
翅

附

2.
菱

雨手を後ろ手に縛り更に捕縄を左腕から
頸にかけ、それを更に右腕に掛けて緊縛
する、縄目が菱形になるから菱と言ふの
である。

必ず縄の上へ〳〵と掛つて居る様縄を掛
ける事を忘れないこと。

引致縄の翅附と同様であるが唯雨肘の所
で更に縄の雨方の端を前に通して充分緊
めて制縛する點が異る。

右の縄の端を右肩の後ろから左縄の端を
左肩の後ろから各々前に廻して前の縄に
二回かけて止め雨端を更に眞中にとつて
後ろに結ぶ。

肘から先は多少の自由が利くから小便等
をせしめるのに便利である。

212

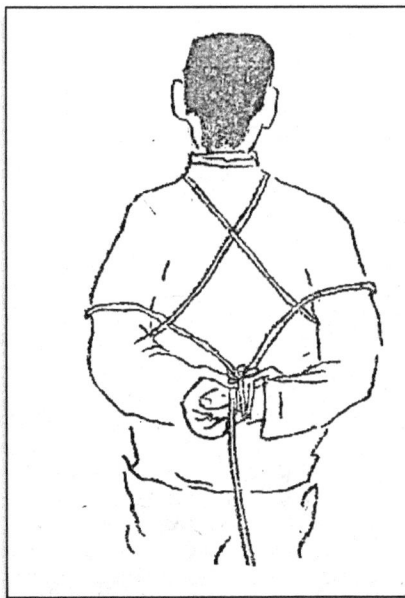

2. Water Chestnut

Tie both of the suspect's hands behind his back. Then wrap the rope around his left arm and around his neck before tying it around his right arm. When finished the lines of the rope will form the shape of a Hishi, Water Chestnut. [24] It is important to remember when tying a person to remember to proceed upward, upward.

---

[24]Hishi 菱 or water chestnut. The shape of the leaves was used as a family seal for various Samurai families.

3. Folded Wings

This tie is basically the same as Arresting Rope : Folded Wings from Part 2,[25] with the main difference being, after tying off both elbows you pass the two ends of the rope forward under the arms and tighten the restraints.

Thread the right end of the rope under the suspect's right shoulder from behind and thread the left end of the rope under the suspect's left shoulder from behind. Wrap each end around the front piece of rope twice and then bring both ends back and tie them off. Then bring both ends to the center and tie a knot.

From the elbows on down the prisoner being transported will have some freedom of movement, so they will be able to urinate and do other tasks by themselves.

---

[25]

Fast Tie version   Prisoner Transport version

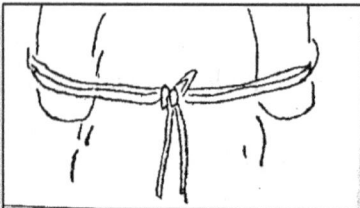

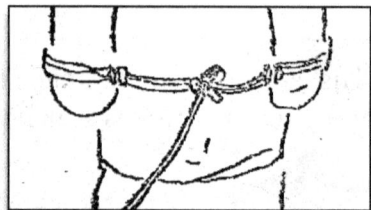

4. Cross-Shaped

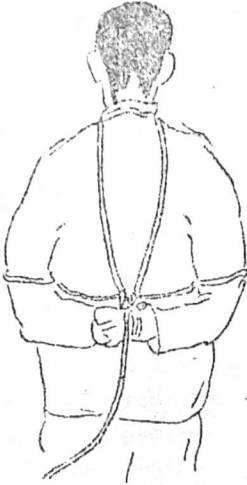
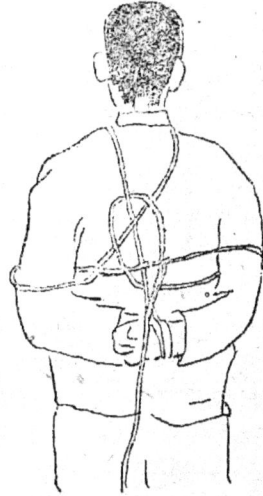

4.
十
文
字

(1)

(2)

(1)

両手を後ろ手に縛し頸にかけたる繩
を左腕から右腕に掛けその端を中央
に通して。

(2)

下に引くと十文字になる、端は良く
止めて更に両手の所に結ぶ。

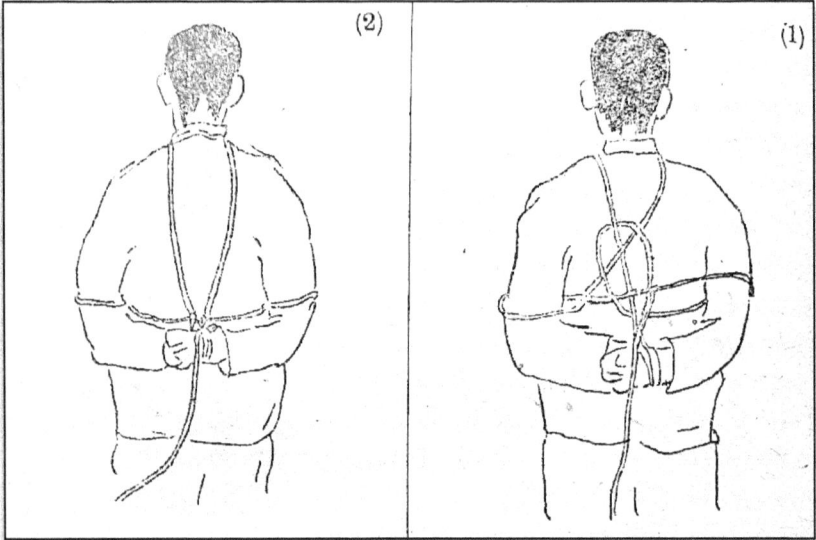

4. Cross-Shaped

1. Bring the suspect's hands behind his back and tie them. Next loop the rope around his neck then around his left arm, followed by his right arm. Then thread that end of the rope through the middle.
2. By pulling the rope straight down the lines of the rope form a Juji, Cross-Shaped, pattern. Ensure that you tie of the end firmly, and make another knot by the hands.

不審者の誰何、尋問
被疑者の同行
留／置場看守

等に關する心得

Things to Remember When Questioning Suspicious Persons, Transporting Suspects and Guarding Suspects in Addition to Other Aspects of Handling Suspects

不審者の誰何尋問、同行、留置場看守
其他被疑者取扱上の心得

不審者の誰何尋問、同行、拘留囚、其他被疑者の取扱は警察上最も重要なる事務に屬し、一度逃走企自殺等の事故發生せんか事前の功績は空しく沒却せられ、且之が回復に甚大なる困難を來すのみならず、社會民衆に及ぼす不安と實害とは決して尠しとせず、警察の威信を失墜すること又最も大なりと謂ふべきなり。

各自に於ても此の種の事故防止に就而は常に努力中のことゝ信ずるも過去の事例に徴するに其の原因は大方油斷と不注意、所謂當務者の職務怠慢に起因すべきもの多く、因つて爾今左記諸點に留意し被疑者は常に逃走、自殺、證據湮滅等の舉に出づること多きものなりとの觀念を持し、之が取扱上充分の工夫を凝し將來此種不祥事の絕對發生せざる樣最全の努力を要す。

◎一、不審尋問

（1）尋問に當りては警察官たることを表示すること

理　由

突然尋問するときは被尋問者をして恐怖の念を抱かしむるのみならず故意に危害を加へしむ

五五

Things to Remember When Questioning Suspicious Persons, Transporting Suspects and Guarding Suspects in Addition to Other Aspects of Handling Suspects

The most important part of police work is questioning suspicious characters, escorting them, handling prisoners and dealing with suspects. If a suspect were able to successfully carry out an escape or commit suicide, then that will become the focus of the public's attention and all the trust and goodwill police have built up will be ignored. Further, not only would that trust be difficult to regain, but it would also harm society as a whole and the citizens would feel less safe. Trust in the police would plummet as a result.

I am sure everyone here realizes that to avoid the types of incidents described above requires that you make a concerted effort as part of your job. For the most part the incidents described above are all the result of errors or a lack of concentration. In other words the reason many of these incidents occurred is the officers in those cases were negligent in their duty.

Thu, nowadays officers should refer to the notes presented on the following pages and understand that it is common for suspects to try to escape, commit suicide, or destroy evidence. Armed with this knowledge officers should seek to adapt it to the situation he finds himself in and strive to prevent these kinds of scandalous events from reoccurring.

Part I
Questioning Suspicious Persons

1. When questioning a suspect first identify yourself as a police officer.

Reason:
If you suddenly begin questioning a person, then not only will the interviewee become fearful, but they would likely consider you an unknown person intending to do them harm. Therefore, before beginning your questions, always identify yourself as a police officer. This will mean good citizens will not be fearful and further it will prevent any misunderstanding.

るの虞なしとせず、故に尋問前必ず警察官たることを表示し良民をして徒に恐怖の念を抱か
しめ又は誤解を招くが如きことなき様注意を要す

（2）　言葉使に注意すること

　理　由

不審尋問は尋問者の主観に依り不審と認めたるものを尋問するに過ぎずして最初より犯人な
りや否やは不明なり、寧ろ不審尋問網にかゝるものは犯罪者よりも善良なる者が其の數に於
て遙に多きを以て言葉使粗暴に流るゝときは徒に相手方を激昂せしめ尋問の目的を達し得ざ
るのみならず之が爲一般民衆をして警察に反感を抱かしむるに至るべし、又時に犯人等は自
己の犯行を蔽はんとして殊更に警察官の言葉使等の攻撃に出づるものあり故に尋問に際して
は努めて叮嚀なる言葉を使ひ被尋問者をして感謝の念を以て尋問に應せしむる様注意を要す

（3）　尋問中は被尋問者の擧動に特に注意すること

　理　由

尋問中は兎角質問應答のみに捉はれ被尋問者の擧動に注意を缺くの結果往々にして危害を加
へられ又は逃走せられたるの例尠からず、故に尋問中は絶えず被尋問者の擧動に注意を拂ひ
萬一にも危害を加へらるゝが如き不覺を取らざる様注意を要す
又犯人は良心の苛責に過ひ其の言動冷静を缺くものなるを以て其の擧動のみを以ても大凡犯

2. Be careful of how you speak

Reason:

The reason you decide to question a suspicious person is entirely due to your subjective decision that a person is acting suspiciously resulting in you questioning them. Initially, you won't know if a person is a criminal or not. If you have deployed a net of police officers to question all the people in an area, most of the people you question will be good upstanding citizens, rather than criminals. Therefore, it is imperative that you do not use rough language.

If you do use coarse language and you are speaking to a tough character, it will likely inflame the situation, thereby preventing you from acquiring the information you seek. Further, by using such language you will erode the authority of the police. In addition, a criminal will be seeking to conceal his crime and use the officer's words to attack the officer. Therefore when questioning a person, always use polite language. When conducting an interview, the person you are interviewing will appreciate the consideration and it will present you with a chance to get the information you need.

（3） 尋問中は被尋問者の舉動に特に注意すること

理　由

尋問中は兎角質問應答のみに捉はれ被尋問者の舉動に注意を鈌くの結果往々にして危害を加へられ又は逃走せられたるの例尠からず、故に尋問中は絶えず被尋問者の舉動に注意を拂ひ萬一にも危害を加へらるゝが如き不覺を取らざる樣注意を要す

又犯人は良心の苛責に遇ひ其の言動冷靜を鈌くものなるを以て其の舉動のみを以ても大凡犯人なりや否やを推知せらるゝものなり、其他犯人は尋問中贓品其の他の證據物件を投棄せんとし或は犯人二人以上なるときは秘密の間に通謀等を爲すの虞あり故に不審尋問に際しては被尋問者の顏色、眼の動き、其の他一舉一動一顰一笑にも細心の注意を拂はざるべからず

3. When interviewing a person, pay particular attention to how they act.

Reason:

When questioning a person, if you only focus on your questions and the interviewee's answers, you will have failed to consider body language. There are more than a few examples of police officers failing to note a person's body language, resulting in a dangerous situation or a suspect successfully escaping. Therefore when questioning a person you should continuously pay attention to their body language. Failing to do so could cause in a dangerous situation and the resulting injury would be attributed to your lack of attention. It is essential that you maintain awareness of this point.

For example, when a criminal comes face to face with a person with a good heart who is chastising them, their lack of calmness and propensity to overreact will allow an officer to make a general assessment of whether or not they are a criminal. Further, a criminal may attempt to dispose of stolen goods or evidence that they committed a crime. If there are two or more criminals, they may try to secretly signal each other, thus during the questioning of suspicious persons, it is imperative that the questioner observe the facial coloring, movement of the eyes as well as expressions like laughs or frowns. An officer should not discount any action or expression by a person he is interviewing.

人なりや否やを推知せらるゝものなり、其他犯人は尋問中臓品其の他の證憑物件を投棄せんとし或は犯人二人以上なるときは秘密の間に通謀等を爲すの虞あり故に不審尋問に際しては被尋問者の顔色、眼の動き、其の他一舉一動一顰笑にも細心の注意を拂はざるべからず

（4）尋問中は特に冷静なる態度を持し論議を避くること

理由
被尋問者中往々にして故らに反問し議論に渉らんとするものあり（例へば不審尋問の根據如何と云ふが如し）又時々犯人等は逃走の機會を作り者は自己の非を蔽はんが爲に故らに反抗的態度に出て警察官を昂奮せしめんとするものあり斯る場合相手方の言動に激發せられ議論に渉るが如きことゝあらんか徒に時間を空費するのみならず時に事端を惹起し若は犯人を逸脱せしむるの虞あるを以て尋問に際しては努めて冷静なる態度を持し所期の目的の達成に努むるを要す

（5）被尋問者と自己の位置に注意すること

理由
被尋問者と自己との位置の關係は被尋問者が逃走を企て或は危害を加ふるに最も不利なる位置に於て被尋問者に接近し其の間何等の動作をも爲す間隙を置かざることを必要とす、而して人は概ね右利なるを以て一人にて尋問する場合は相手の右を制する爲被尋問者の右方に接

五七、

4. When questioning a person it is imperative that you remain calm and avoid arguing.

Reason:

It is not uncommon for the person being interviewed to react with questions of their own in an attempt to start a debate (For example: Why did you think I was suspicious? Why are you questioning me?) Sometimes suspects will do this to give themselves a chance to escape. They may also try to conceal their violation of the law by adopting an argumentative manner to irritate an officer. If an officer continues to engage in verbal escalation with a suspect not only will the time spent with the suspect be wasted but it may provoke an incident. It can also give a criminal a chance to escape. Thus it is important that you maintain a calm attitude while interviewing and work towards achieving your goal.

5. Be aware of how you position yourself in relation to the person you are interviewing.

Reason:

When you are interviewing a person, you should be aware of how you are positioned in relation to the interviewee. It is essential that you approach from an angle and maintain a distance from your subject that makes it difficult for him to escape or to do violence. Generally speaking, people are right-handed so when approaching a person to interview, the officer should try to control their subject's right side so that is the direction you should approach from.

If you are interviewing two people you should always position yourself so that one of the subjects is standing either behind the one you are interviewing, or to that person's right. It is imperative that you watch the second person carefully as you interview the first.

し二人にて尋問するときは一人は絶えず被尋問者の後方若は右方に位置して絶えず其の舉動に注意し他の一人が尋問に當るを適當なりとす

（6）　被尋問者の携帯品を取調ぶること

理　由

尋問方法としては出發地、行先地、用件、住所、氏名、年齡其の他の口頭尋問を行ひ容疑の點の有無を究明することも勿論一の手段たるも被尋問者の携帯品の取調べを缺くべからず、即ち口頭にては巧妙に遁避し得るとするも一度携帯品を取調ぶるときは應答と矛盾を生じ又贓品其の他の證據物件を發見され遂に辯解の餘地なきに至るものなり、又携帯品の取調べは容疑の點を發見するのみならず尋問者の自衛上に於ても亦缺くべからざるものにして之が取調べを爲さず又は取調べ粗漏の結果懷中せる短刀其の他の戎兇器を以て危害を加へられたるの例決して稀なりとせず、故に尋問に際しては先づ其の携帯品中特に戎兇器等の有無を確め たる上尋問に着手する樣心掛くべし

（7）　不審の點を徹底的に究明すること

理　由

被尋問者は假令犯人に非ずと雖も質問に對する應答は可成之を簡にし努めて尋問の點を殘さらんとするを常とし容易に疑問の點を發見し得ざるものなるを以て疑問の點發見したると

五八

6. Examining a suspect's goods.

Reason:

During your questioning you will of course ask about where a person came from, where they're headed, along with their address, name, age and so on. Clearly another way to confirm whether or not a person is a suspect is to examine what items they are carrying. This is a step that is essential to a thorough investigation.

For example, a person may be quite deft at answering questions and evading the truth, however one look at the items they are carrying will reveal inconsistencies with their previous statements.

If you find stolen goods or other evidence on the suspect, then that person will have lost the ability to explain away their movements. Further, when examining the items carried by a suspect it is possible to find something that implicates them in a crime, in addition it also serves to protect the officer conducting the interview. Thus searching the suspect is an essential step.

Neglecting this step is very dangerous as a suspect could have a short sword or other dangerous weapon on his person which he could use to injure you. Such situations are not uncommon. In conclusion, when questioning a person you should always check the items they are carrying to ensure there are no weapons before beginning your questions.

7. You must work tenaciously to discover the source of your suspicion.

Reason:

While the person you are interviewing may not be a suspect, you may notice they do not seem to be answering your questions completely. If your questions are not being answered, you will have trouble finding inconsistencies in a person's statements. It is important that you thoroughly investigate any small inconsistency you detect in an interviewee's answers until you have a definitive answer. It is essential that you do not ignore the subtle signs of doubt you feel in a suspect's statement or fail to follow up on a suspicious inconsistency in a suspect's story.

きは微細なる疑問の點と雖も之を徹底的に究明し始めて所期の目的を達し得らるゝなり、故に微細なる疑問なりとして之を閑却し又は疑問の點を發見するも之が究明の勞を厭ふが如きことなきを要す

（8） 携帯品の取調べに際しては一應其の品目數量等を聽取したる上取調ぶるを可とす

理　由

携帯品にして自己の所有物なるに於ては其の品目數量等を知悉し居るべき等なるを以て若し之が答辯と實際と符合せざる場合に於ては其處に容疑の點を發見し得らるゝものなればなり

（9） 携帯品の取調は可成本人をして檢せしむること

理　由

携帯品を取調ぶるときは被審問者に對する注意力を缺き逃走若は危害を加へらるゝ虞なしとせず、故に携帯品の取調べは一應戎兇器等の有無を取調べたる上は可成本人をして檢せしむるを可とす

（10） 被審問者の詐言に迷はされざること

理　由

被審問者にして審問を豫期せざるときは狼狽の餘り其の答辯矛盾を發見され易きも豫め之を豫期し居るときは巧に詐言を弄するものなるを以て假令被審問者の答辯等に矛盾の點なき場

8. When examining the items a suspect is carrying, question them regarding the number, amount or other related question.

Reason:

Since the objects found on a person are ostensibly their own, they should be able to answer questions specific questions related to them like the number or volume. *If the two halves of the ticket do not match…* as the saying goes, you will have found an inconsistency in their statement.

9. When inspecting the items a suspect is carrying be sure to maintain a watch on the suspect.

Reason:

When examining the items carried by a person you are interviewing, it is imperative to watch the interviewee carefully as failing to do so could mean they escape or attempt violence. Thus while it is important to check for weapons or other dangerous objects it is also essential you watch over the suspect carefully.

10. Don't allow a person's lies to mislead you.

Reason:

If the responses you are getting to your questions are unexpectedly confused and doubtful, take that into consideration and deftly use the interviewee's attempt at deceit as a device to find the information you need.

For example, you can pretend that you don't find any inconsistencies in an interviewee's responses and continue to ask questions regarding a certain point. Or you can create a fictional person or place and use that to continue your line of questioning. There are a variety of angles to approach this situation from however you need to be tenacious in pursuit of the point of doubt in an interviewee's statement.

◎二、被疑者の同行

（1）同行に際しては更に身體捜檢を精密に行ふこと

理由

犯人又は不審者の同行前身體捜檢を怠り又は之が精密を缺きたるの結果同行の途中に於て危害を加へられ又は證據物件を投棄せられたるの例尠からず故に不審尋問中一應身體の捜檢を了したりとて其の儘とせず更に同行前精密なる身體捜檢を行ふの要あり

（2）現行犯人には必ず捕縄を施すこと

理由

現行犯人にして引致せらるゝ場合特に温順を装ひ逃走せざることを誓ひ施錠を免かれんとするものあるも之等の多くは逃走の餘地を作らんが爲の口實に過ぎざるを以て特別の事情存せざる限り必ず施錠するを要す

（3）戎兇器及證據物件は自ら携帯すること

理由

同行の途中は敏活なる行動を執り得る樣被尋問者の携帯品は可成被尋問者に携帯せしむるを

合と雖も直に之を信ずるが如きことなく尋問中同一事項を重ねて質問し或は架空の人物若は場所等を設けて質問する等各種の方面より追求して疑問の點を發見するに努むべし

六〇

Part II
Transporting a Suspect

1. When preparing to escort a prisoner, do a second detailed body search

Reason:

If you are escorting a criminal or a suspicious person and you fail to search them or do not conduct thorough inspection, then you may end up with a dangerous situation during transport. Also, it is not uncommon for suspects to try and dispose of evidence along the way. Therefore, even though you searched the suspicious person as part of your interview, a prudent officer should conduct another thorough search of their body before transporting them.

2. Any criminal you arrest should be secured with rope.

Reason:

When arresting a suspect at the scene, many will, quite convincingly, promise that they will not try to escape in order to avoid being tied up. In many cases this is a ploy to allow the suspect a chance to escape while being transported. Therefore unless there are extenuating circumstances, all suspects should be restrained before transport.

3. Any weapons, potentially dangerous items or evidence should be carried by the officer.

Reason:

In order to transport the interviewee in a rapid and orderly fashion, the officer may decide it is appropriate to allow the interviewee to carry all their own belongings, or the interviewee may request to carry their own dangerous objects or evidence. This is liable to create a dangerous situation and may lead to the destruction of evidence.

適當とするも戎兇器又は證據物件は同行者自ら携帯するを要す、之れ危險の發生竝證據の湮滅を防がんが爲なり

（４）同行の途中は先行せざること

理由

同行の途中被同行者に先行するときは逃走せられ又は危害を加へらるべの機會多きを以て常に後方より適當の間隔を保ち同行するを可とす

（５）同行時には可成河岸崖端其の他危險なる道筋を避くること

理由

河岸又は崖端等を同行の際犯人より打落され又は自ら河中に飛込み崖下等に飛降り逃走を企てたる例尠からず故に止むことを得ざる場合の外此等危險の場所の通行は之を避くるを要す

（６）同行は可成人混中を避くること

理由

人混に紛れ逃走せらるゝ虞あるのみならず被同行者の體面を重ずるが爲なり

（７）被同行者の詐術に陷らざること

理由

犯人は往々にして同行の途中假病を装ひ又は用便を訴ふる等凡ゆる詐術を弄し逃走を企てん

六二

4. When transporting a suspect, never walk in front.

Reason:

When escorting a suspect if you walk in front, this creates innumerable chances for the suspect to escape or attempt to do you harm. The standard method is to walk behind the suspect at a suitable distance.

5. When transporting a suspect, be sure to avoid areas near high river embankments, cliffs or other such dangerous places.

Reason:

You should avoid transporting suspects past rivers or cliffs since the criminal may try to knock you into one or the other. There is also the risk the suspect may try to jump into the river or off a precipice in order to escape.

6. When escorting a suspect avoid passing through crowded areas.

Reason:

If you escort a suspect through a crowd, not only does this give the suspect the chance to escape, but it can also further damage the suspect's dignity.

7. Don't allow yourself to be deceived by the person you are escorting.

Reason:

Criminals frequently feign illness whilst being transported, claim to need to use the bathroom or use other such pretext in order to facilitate their escape. If, while escorting a suspect, you are forced to allow them to use the bathroom, then be sure to keep the door open and observe the criminal carefully. Be vigilant to not fall for some trick.

とするものなるを以て仮令止を得ず用便を許すが如き場合と雖も扉を開放し厳重之を監視する等犯人の詐術に陥らざる様注意を要す

（8）　汽車、電車、自動車等の乗降に注意すること

理由

汽車、電車、自動車等の乗物にて犯人を同行するときは其の乗降時に間隙を生じ易く逃走されたるの實例も尠からざるに付二人にて同行するときは犯人を挾み一人にて同行するときは後方より犯人に接して乗降するを適當とす

（9）　自殺を企てられざる様注意すること

理由

同行の途中犯人は往々毒劇薬等を嚥下し又は其の他の方法に依り自殺を企つる場合あり故に同行前の身體捜檢に際し自殺に用ふる物件等の有無を細密調査するは勿論同行の途中に於ても其の他の方法に依り自殺を企てしむるが如きことなき様常に深甚の注意を拂ふべし

（10）　警察署の入口又は其の附近に到りたるときは特に注意を要す

理由

警察署の入口又は其の附近に到るときは同行者に於て緊密を缺くの虞あるに反し犯人は逃走せんが爲最後の手段を講ずるの虞あり、從來此の種事例決して尠からざるに付嚴に留意を要す

六二

8. Be careful when embarking or disembarking a locomotive, trolley, automobile or other conveyance.

Reason:

   When escorting a person using locomotives, trolleys, automobiles or other such conveyances it is not uncommon for a criminal to try and use the opening created when entering or exiting a vehicle as a chance to escape. Therefore it is prudent for two officers to escort a criminal, sandwiching him in between you and the other officer. If an officer is transporting a prisoner alone, then stand directly behind the prisoner when embarking or disembarking.

9: Be vigilant if the suspect seems like they are planning to commit suicide.

Reason:

   Frequently suspects that are being escorted will try to drink some sort of poison or other drug. Or they may try another way to commit suicide. Thus it is important to search their body carefully when doing your initial interrogation to locate anything that could be used to commit suicide. Clearly, even if you do not find anything on them, you should maintain your vigilance while escorting the suspect, being aware of anything along the way that the suspect could use to harm themselves.

10. Pay particular attention to the suspect as you approach the door to the police station or its environs.

Reason:

   When arriving at the entrance to the police station with the prisoner, your attention may lapse. This will give the criminal a last chance to escape. This situation is not uncommon, so it is essential that officers remain vigilant.

（11） 被疑者を警察署へ同行したる場合は必ず責任者に引渡すこと

理　由

被疑者を同行したるときは當直主任者又は留置場看守に完全に身柄を引渡し同行理由を報告して始めて其の責任の全部を完了するものにして過去の事例に徴するに之が完全なる引渡しを爲さゞる爲折角同行したる被疑者に逃走せられたる等の事例あり之が完全引渡しを爲し萬遺憾なきを期するの要あり

◎三、留置場看守

（1）　留置人の身體檢査は嚴重に行ふこと

理　由

留置場に入房せしむるに際しては最も嚴重に身體檢査をするの要あり之が粗漏の爲兇器、證據物件等を發見し得ず爲に逃走、自殺、證據湮滅等を企圖せられたる事例決して尠なからざるに付嚴重なる身體檢査を爲すの要あり

（2）　各監房の施錠は最も完全なるを要すること

理　由

勤務に狎れ各監房の施錠を不完全にし或は小使等に留置場の開閉を委せて施錠不充分の爲め逃走せられたる例多きを以て留置場及監房の開閉は必ず看守者自ら之をなし以て最も完全な

六三

11. After transporting a suspect to the police station, you must hand the suspect over to the person in charge.

Reason:

The responsibility for the suspect an officer is transporting does not end until you hand the suspect over to the person in charge at the station or the warden of the jail and fill out a report regarding why you are escorting the suspect.

There have been situations where the hand-off of suspects has been ambiguous and has led to escapes. Therefore it is an outrageous violation to not properly complete the hand-off process.

Part III
Guarding Prisoners

1. Conduct an extremely thorough search of prisoners

Reason:

Before placing a prisoner in a cell be sure that you conduct a thorough search of their body. If, through inattention, you do not discover a weapon or a piece of evidence in the prisoner's possession, they may use that to escape or commit suicide. They may also destroy crucial evidence. This is not an infrequent occurrence, so it is essential that you search a prisoner's body thoroughly.

2. Each of the doors at the prison should be locked securely and confirmed locked.

Reason:

There are many examples of prisoners escaping due to guards presuming that the doors to each of the cells in a prison are locked or due to laxness regarding the doors to the restroom. The jailer should personally check not only the doors to the jail itself, but the doors of each cell. Failing to ensure all doors are completely locked in unconscionable.

る施錠を爲し遺憾なきを要す

（3） 留置人の擧動に注意すること

理　由

看守者は常に留置人の擧動に最も綿密なる注意を拂ひ、降房及房外者等に對する通謀、連絡等を防止すると共に自殺、逃走等を企圖せらる丶の餘地なからしむる機細心の注意を要し尙在房者の健康に留意し罹病者の早期發見に努むること

（4） 取調主任者と看守者とは常に緊密なる連絡を保持すること

理　由

重要事犯又は著名人物の關係する犯罪にして自己の自白が他に重大影響を及ぼし又は其の他の關係に依り相當自責に藉られ自殺其の他の自害行爲に出づる場合有之を以て常に之等事犯關係者の取調べに際しては取調主任者と看守者とは緊密なる連絡を保ち之が失態なき樣充分留意するを要す

（5） 留置人出入の場合は必ず二人立會ふこと

理　由

留置人は往々逃走の目的を以て假病を裝ひ用便を訴ふる等の凡ゆる詐術を用ひ看守人を欺罔して房外に出て看守人の隙を窺ひ看守人に對し暴行、毆打、絞首、其の他の暴力を加へ看守

六四

238

3. Pay attention to the movements of the prisoners.

Reason:

The jailer should always keep the prisoners under close observation. In addition to keeping prisoners from plotting with prisoners in their own cell or other cells, a jailer should watch out for prisoners planning suicide attempts as well as escape attempts. In addition to these measures, you should also pay attention to the health of your prisoners and seek aid quickly if they contract an illness.

4. It is imperative that there is clear communication between the head investigator and the jailers.

Reason:

If there is a case of particular severity or if the criminal case involves a high-profile person, anything you say could greatly influence the case. Due to other related factors the information you leak could lead you could face severe reprimand. It could result in suicide or other kinds of self-harm. Therefore when communicating information regarding a high-profile case, be sure that the information is only shared with the head investigator and the jailer.

5. Whenever a prisoner is entering or exiting a cell, there should be two guards present.

Reason:

Prisoners will often feign illness as a pretext for part of an escape plan. A jailer should be alert for this and any other kind of craftiness on the part of the prisoners.

人を人事不省に陥らしめて逃走したる事例あり之が出入には必ず看守者二名以上立會ひたる

上之を爲す様注意を要す、留置人を取調室其の他の場所へ同行する場合は決して先行せざる

こと

（6）　被疑者を留置場より刑事室其の他の場所へ同行する時は之に先行せず且つ下命者に確實

に引渡すこと

理　由

（被疑者の同行（4）及（11）參照）

六五

6. When transporting a suspect from jail to the detective's office or other place, do not walk ahead of the prisoner. Further, ensure you transfer the prisoner to the proper person as ordered.

Reason:
(See Transporting Suspects entries 4 and 11)

昭和十六年十二月一日印刷
昭和十六年十二月五日發行

神奈川縣警察部警務刑事課編纂

（非賣品）

印刷者　横濱市中區花咲町一丁目四十九番地　江森八十吉

印刷所　横濱市中區花咲町一丁目四十九番地　江森印刷所　電話長者町四五九七番

Published December 5th in the 16th Year of Showa
(1941)
Kanagawa Prefectural Police Department
Yokohama City
(Not for Sale)

www.ingramcontent.com/pod-product-compliance
Lightning Source LLC
Chambersburg PA
CBHW072122270326
41931CB00010B/1638